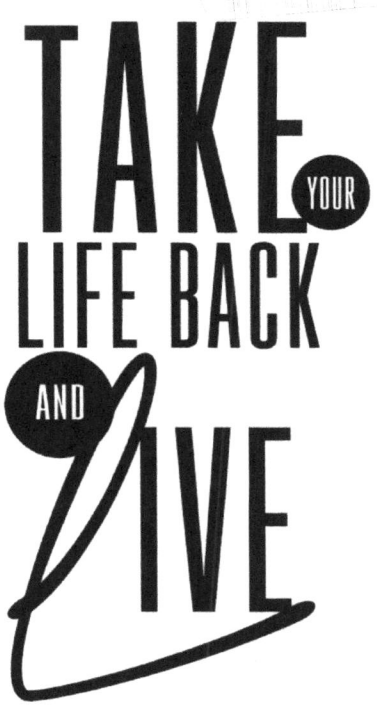

DR. ANE MERCER

Copyright © 2017 Dr. Ane Mercer

All rights reserved.

ISBN-13: 978-0-692-96619-8

"Dr. Ane Mercer's riveting redeeming *book Take Your Life Back and Live* is a powerfully confronting construct that courageously exposes the origins, repercussions, and lasting damage of the SIN OF ADULTERY in the church. Dr. Mercer's courage and transparency compels believers to trace the origin of this secret societal struggle as she carefully with strategic biblical principles routes readers to restoration and recovery."

Tonya Hall, Pastor
Victory Way Christian Center
Jacksonville, Florida

"*TYLB&L* embellishes the secrets life of adultery and is a very well done instrument of ministry. It is so needed and clearly addresses the subject that is most times avoided. It brings revenant insight and a powerful message. Thanks for allowing your pain to become a pulpit of healing and hope for others."

Bishop Carolyn Boston Love, Pastor
One Church of Jacksonville
Truth Bible University, President
Jacksonville, Florida

"Sometimes two people form a passionate yet dysfunctional connection that *feels right* but is all WRONG! In that moment, they are blinded by selfishness. The truth is that LOVE HEALS! Dr. Ane Mercer courageously confronts her own broken places and dares to give us an all-access glimpse into the life of being the other woman. Whether you have been involved in an affair, or are the collateral damage of one, this book just might be the catalyst for your healing too."

Dr. Vikki Johnson
Chaplain, Speaker, Author
#SoulWealth, Creator

"To be sure, every vessel that is used to facilitate the work of emotional healing in others must possess five qualities: AVAILABILITY, COURAGE, HUMILITY, TRANSPARENCY, and VULNERABILITY. True healers have the uncanny and unique ability to take the narrative of personal pain—pain that is sometimes self-inflicted—and offer it to the public as a medicinal remedy for the mending of a broken heart, and the soothing of a sick soul. In *Take Your Life Back & Live*, Dr. Ane Mercer equips the reader to rise from the ashes of despair and disappointment, and encourages them to ascend to a dimension of renewal and restoration that God has made available to all humanity. This is a MUST read!"

Bishop Kevin Long, Pastor
Temple Church International
Charlotte, North Carolina

DEDICATION

These pages are the sentiments of my heart with memories of so many people down through the years who encouraged me to tell my story. To my children (Team Ane) Jamal, Bre 'Onna, Moo and the Twins Amar and Ashton – whose love encourages me to always be the best and beckons me to my future. I am also thankful to my Sisterhood who supported me through my journey. They are amazing. And last but not least, I am so grateful to Bishop Clinton and Lady Mary House who gave me the strength to be me and to never be ashamed of what the Lord has done in my life.

Contents

	Introduction	i.
1.	Roots of Reality	5
2.	The Spot	21
3.	Secrets Are Not Sassy	35
4.	Meet the Players (Provocative, Prolific, and Passionate)	51
5.	The Breaking Point	97
6.	Through the Eyes of the Other Woman	113
7.	The Recovery	123
8.	A Better Way Forward	127
9.	One-on-One Accountability	137
10.	On the Other Side of Ugly	143
11.	Sex on Another Level	149
12.	The Day I Decided to Die on the Inside	159

ACKNOWLEDGEMENTS

To my little sister Eva and only brother Donald Coward Jr. – you are simply two of the greatest gifts He could have given to me. Thank you for allowing me to live, heal and stand in your love for me.

To my mom, Cathy DuBose, hats off to you – I love you for being assigned as my mother.

To my father Donald Coward Sr. – thanks for speaking greatness over my life.

To my spiritual mother and father – you assured me that I can succeed!

To my Uncle Cedric – thank you for being my strength. I love you so much.

To Mitchell C. Payden – the best worker on the face of the planet – for coming to find me and making my dream of becoming an author come true. Thank you for being my voice of support through the years. You are the bomb! This would not have been possible without you.

Thank you for all who labored with me on *Taking My Life Back*. You are phenomenal.

INTRODUCTION

I was born to be great. That's clear to me now. But it can be hard to see that when you're mired in the consequences of bad decisions. Whether you made them because of low self-esteem or because you were in full-scale rebellion – or because the one led to the other – you can find yourself in such a mess of your own making that it's hard to believe God called you to greatness.

And it's even harder to believe He can still get you there in spite of everything you've done to get yourself off course. Especially when that involves adultery.

I don't like knowing so much about adultery, and having that knowledge come from first-hand experience – from every conceivable angle. But we can only live life from the present going forward. I could pretend these things never happened, or I can accept that I've learned a great deal from my mistakes.

And that I can help people like you by sharing what I've learned. That's what I want to do. And that's why I've written this book.

People will oftentimes not understand your course to discovery and the journey it takes to unfold your inner being. Most times it's frightening, and someone like myself will battle with the what-ifs and the domino effect of the onion being peeled. But nevertheless, it is apparent that many of us have a similar story.

Every one of us was born for a specific reason. I understand now that I survived to be the encouragement for someone else to soar. I have learned that healing is a place where most people dream to go. But they dare not take the proper steps. Inner healing is very painful, because more often than not it involves other people's issues, hangups and emotional baggage.

Life never comes with an instruction manual, but it will give you a story.

Throughout the journey known as my life, I have learned that I was never a mistake. It was an abandoned root in the soil of my being that caused me to become a very bent young girl, lady and woman. Identifying my pain was the most intimate place of my discovery, but it took, and is continuing to take, a lot of work.

I had to change some things that provided temporary comfort for my issues. I had to re-evaluate my friends, acquaintances, spiritual connections and guard myself even from some family members.

In this book you will see some of the very real dangers of life, and the consequences of making the wrong choices concerning those dangers. Regardless of how you perceive yourself at times, your lack of accepting the "real you" prevents you from gaining victory over your issues.

This book is a must-read for you, your friends, your family members and anyone else who has found themselves in the web of adultery. Although this lifestyle has long been a part of our society and affects all social classes, it is now the most common cause of families ending in devastation. It is separating marriages, damaging our children, bringing reproach upon our government officials and causing many of our spiritual leaders to stumble in open shame.

From the White House to the ghetto, we all – in some form – have been touched by individuals who have experienced this scourge or have become victims of it.

There is a larger issue at work here as well. Society is very focused on success, but we never have a plan for failure. We never go through life preparing to get into anything that will damage the plan that God has mapped for our lives. We live to reach our destination, but we're not prepared for detours, and once we find ourselves off course we don't know how to get back on because we never thought we would have to.
I'd gotten way off course. I found out how to get back on. If everyone understood what I've learned, it could make all the difference in the world.

Now I am not so delusional as to think that this book will change the world. But I have every confidence it could impact a generation of people who would embrace it as a resource to help them reach their place of release.

The lifestyle of adultery is a major sign that there is a problem, a void, some dissatisfaction. It's time for us to stop blaming someone else for our decision to choose this path. I know there are people who have affairs and end up marrying the other man or woman and they live happily ever after – or so it seems. But I am a firm believer that you reap what you sow. Fantasy and marriage are two different playgrounds.

As I was thinking about writing this book, I couldn't help but think about the many propositions I receive from men who are married. Now that I have paid a tremendous price to become free, I dare not return to a life that taints my identity and brings demise to my character.

One thing I have learned, however, is lust can never be

fulfilled. The path of adultery is filled with highs and lows, and it is paved with the manipulation of another person's vulnerability.

This revelation caused me to go on an emotional rollercoaster. I experienced ups and downs, twist and turns, until the consequences of my actions came back like a locomotive, and all my mistakes were reflected back at me like a mirror!

When I came through this process, I was so determined that it was time to take my life back and live. It was, and has been, a journey.
But I did it!

In this book, I speak the truth about life and the paralyzing effect of having too many options. In the upcoming chapters, find out the secrets and the allure of adultery, and what you can do to avoid making the mistakes that many people before you have made.

One thing I have learned is that you can share what you know, but you can't make another person heed the warnings. Even if they know you're right, they may still disregard what they've learned and do what they want.

My job is to share. I pray that you will heed. Maybe between you, me and God, we can turn my experiences into a blessing for you.

CHAPTER ONE

The Roots of Reality

"We do not grow absolutely, chronologically. We grow sometimes in one dimension, and not in another; unevenly. We grow partially. We are relative. We are mature in one realm, childish in another. The past, present, and future mingle and pull us backward, forward, or fix us in the present. We are made up of layers, cells, constellations."

— Anais Nin

You Cannot Properly Heal What You Refuse to Properly Confront

There are so many of us who want to glorify our success stories and brag about all the luxuries of life but few of us are able to look at ourselves in the mirror and deal with our danger zones. We all know what those places are – they are the places that drive us into cycles, attracting different people who are carrying the same spirit of polluted influence.

I know that no one can make you do anything. But I will say, and I often emphasize this to so many women who were and are in this deceptive lifestyle like I was: The one that holds your ear navigates your heart!

Many of us do not even realize that every house was built with "plugs", and we know there are certain things you do not stick in an outlet or it will electrocute you. The same rule goes for our personal lives. We were made as humans to have outlets in our lives and only certain people are supposed to plug into them.

Early on, I learned that wisdom did not necessarily come with age. My life has been a journey, and at every turn I am discovering who I am. I am healing my way back to myself. I am redefining my options, and I am coming into loving me more than anything. Not selfishly, but understanding that until I learn how to love myself, I will always make the same mistakes.

The Beginning...

One morning when I was four years old, my mom was getting us ready to leave. She was going to work and I was going to school. As this was happening, my great-grandmother called (yes, I remember this like it was today) and said, "Cathy, please do not take Ane to school today." Having had a dream of a horrible car wreck, she added, "I don't feel right in my spirit."

My mother replied, "Ms. Wheelwright, just pray for us."

On this particular morning, I was in the front seat with my mother, and three of my mom's friends were in the back seat. As we were going up Chapman Highway in Knoxville, Tennessee, a speeding car came out of nowhere and slammed into us. I went through the side window and my mother went through the windshield. None of the other passengers in the car were injured.

It was a deep, dark morning of fear, and as a little girl, seeing my mother covered in blood on the ground was traumatizing. All I could remember hearing was the paramedics saying, "We're losing her!"

My mother experienced severe head trauma. They allowed me to ride with her in the ambulance, and I recall them working on her. I kept crying "Mama, please don't die!" I witnessed my mother fight to survive and I really believe my pleas to her kept her fighting to live.

When they took her back behind those swinging doors, all I said was, "God, if you are real, don't let my mama die." She survived, but my mother, who is a very beautiful woman, and who then had long beautiful hair, was now bald on one side with bandages wrapped around her head.

I will never forget the long road of recovery for her. It was hard on our family but I stayed right there beside her. You would think that during such a difficult time our family would be brought closer together. You would be wrong.

My childhood was a far cry from the beloved Cosby show. My parents would fight each other with car jacks. My dad would grab butcher knives and try to cut my mom. I still have the scar to remind me of when my hand got in the way of the blade.

One day my dad hit the wound on my mom's head. The scream that came out of her frightened me so much that I ran and held her as I told him to leave her alone. But the arguing never stopped, it just continued. My mom would discover vodka bottles hidden in the toilet bowl. Our cars were getting repossessed, and my mother would cry.

All of these traumatic and eventful situations framed my world and taught me that fighting was a way to survive. This is not an excuse for making bad choices. They are simply some of the experiences I had to confront within me many years later in order to heal the root of bitterness that had formed in my soul.

My father was an entertainer. He loved being the star

of the show! I think he got that from James Brown, of whom he was a huge fan. Mr. Brown owned a radio station in my hometown of Knoxville, and whenever a James Brown song would come on that station, my father would grab his microphone and sing his heart out.

He later formed a group called Donnie and the Last, which was probably his greatest effort to follow in the footsteps of the famous Godfather of Soul.

I would watch my daddy with stars in my eyes and be amazed at his doing the splits and the ability to glide across the stage with his sandy brown hair and beautiful sage-green eyes. He was short, but had a big, melodious voice. My father loved performing and he did it well.

I remember vividly when "Climbing the Stairway to Heaven" came out and my dad told me to stand on his feet so he could teach me how to dance. He looked at me and said, "Ane, I will be the first man to show you how a man should treat his woman. I am going to teach you how to dance at your prom and at your wedding."

He repeatedly confirmed to me that no man would love me more than he did. And because of that, I was daddy's little girl and I wanted to model everything I did after my dad's performances. He would have me perform all of Donna Summers's greatest hits, and would insist that one day the world would know my name. He would say, "God is going to use your mouth and I am going to be right there to cheer you on."

But even after all of those words of encouragement from my dad, his greatest lesson to me was not what he said but what he did.

My parents fought all the time, but in the midst of building me up as his daddy's girl, his words and practices were not in alignment with his message to me. However, I didn't care. I loved my daddy. I witnessed my mom and dad fight like cats and dogs. I saw knives and bottles being thrown, and once, my mom tried to run my father over with the car.

He would retaliate by hitting my mom and locking her out of the house. I was privy to so many unhealthy emotions, but I loved my daddy. My dad had friends over that looked like females (what would be called transgendered today) but I loved my daddy. My father had a friend that would ask me to sit on his lap and he would touch me. But because he was one of my dad's friends, I could not tell because I loved my daddy.

One day my mom came in and told me that my dad was gone. He had moved out and was going to live in Los Angeles, California. I did not understand. How could he just abandon his little girl?

I remember hearing my mom cry and ask God how she was going to take care of us. She cried so hard and it led me to make up my mind that no man would ever break me like my dad broke my mom.

That day, something left from my heart and I felt a breaking in my soul. I started feeling emotions of guilt and shame, and like leaves changing to a beautiful myriad of colors in autumn in preparation for winter, the love and adulation I felt for my father slowly turned into hate and bitterness. I wanted to fight him! All of my dreams of dancing at my prom and my wedding with my daddy turned to nightmares.

I never understood how my dad could just walk away without saying goodbye.

Broken House

The foundation of my emotional house was broken, and from that point on everything that began to go up was built upon brokenness. I erected walls; I became very withdrawn and would go into my closet or hide under the bed to find solitude.

So now my house was being built, my walls were up and in those walls were outlets and they were on fire! My temper became like a short inside an outlet. I sparked on everything and everybody.

The ultimate insult to injury came when my mom approached me and gave me a talk I did not comprehend at the time because I was only ten. She said it was time that I grew up and help her take care of my little brother, who was, and still is, the most precious thing to my heart. And because I love my brother, I willingly agreed. But I didn't know I was exchanging my childhood for premature adulthood.

I became my father's replacement. I lived a role and had responsibilities I could not fill. Those were a pair of shoes that were not supposed to be worn by a child. I grew up feeling obligated to take care of my brother and all the while I did not know that I was building a No Trespass sign to my heart.

Over the next few years, I was determined not to allow anyone to come onto the property of my spirit, my soul and especially my life. I dreamt of running outside and playing. I wished I had the luxury of playing with Barbie and Ken, and I wanted to use my Easy Bake Oven, enjoy tea parties and eat cookies. But because of my responsibilities to my brother, I was unable to do any of those things. Most people I know would have feelings of resentment toward their sibling, but I never have. The only thing I was beckoned to do was to love him, and most of all, keep him safe. The last thing I wanted him exposed to was the hurt and pain I was experiencing.

By this time, it had been years since my father left and the only way we knew him was through a child support check which was few and far between. My mother became so frustrated. She would call him everything but a child of God. In my early years of development, I didn't know that not having my father around would open me up to a world for which I was not mentally or physically prepared.

If I could make a plea right here, it would simply be this: Men, please be in your children's lives! There is a place in all of us that we cannot build as we should without a father's help. When fathers do not tap in – and pour in – to that place, children are left to fantasize about what having a father might be like. This is when they create images so perfect that no one can live up to them. They are a substitute for the real love and guidance they should have had, and they ultimately lead to disappointment. Men: we do not expect you to be perfect, but we do need you to be there.

Allow me to emphasize that I am not by any means talking about fathers who sexually, verbally or physically abuse their children. I am talking about a healthy relationship between a parent and their child.

Lost Innocence

My mother was under so much pressure from raising my brother and I alone that she wrote a letter to my father and told him that she could not keep taking care of us. Now, let me emphasize that my mom was a GREAT provider for her children. Her methods and relational skills may have been off, but I have learned to appreciate her for what she did for us. My mother did a great job with certain things: Our houses were nice, and our clothes were always beautiful. She just did not know how to "parent" us. She did the best she could with the knowledge she had.

Having determined that neither parent was in a position to care for us, my parents came up with a plan to send us to Cincinnati, Ohio, to stay with my grandmother.

This decision would forever change the direction of my life.

That summer would be a pivotal point in my emotional dysfunction. My brother and I went to live with my father's mother, and she was angry and felt like she owed it to him to take care of his kids because she did not raise her first four children. To me, it seemed like she kept us out of guilt.

Now, my grandmother had a huge home, and it seemed like everybody lived there: aunts, cousins, in-and-outs, etc. It was a miserable place to be, especially after I found out the history between the Knoxville children and the Ohio children. Every family has secrets and we were told, "What goes on in our house stays in our house."

It was there that I experienced my first sexual encounter.

I was already afraid, because even though these people were family, they were unknown to me, like strangers. One night, my aunt came into my room and got into bed with me. She touched me with her hands and her mouth. I knew it was wrong by nature but I didn't know how to handle it. At the age of ten, I knew that boys and girls did things to each other, but I had never heard of girls and girls together.

Under threats against my little brother, I kept quiet while she would perform oral sex on me, which I didn't understand at all. If I didn't let her do this, she would force me to walk outside in bare feet because she knew I was deathly afraid of water bugs and critters (which their yard was infested with, by the way.) Shortly after that, a similar incident happened with my uncle. I felt unprotected, uncovered and alone. I asked myself, "Why is this happening to me?" I was a little girl!

Ashamed, degraded and in physical pain, I got up and dragged myself to my ugly room with the gross pink walls where I would lie across my bed and cry. I kept saying, "I want to go home," but no one heard my cries of despair. I prayed and asked God to let me die. I didn't want to wake up, and I didn't want to go to sleep. I didn't want to talk because I didn't know how to explain the awful things that had happened to me. I felt like my beauty was a curse – I hated that I had brown hair and distinctive green eyes like my dad. They set me apart – especially in the black community. I hated that my smile was beautiful, so I just stopped smiling.

One day, we were outside and a huge cloud formed in the sky. The smell of rain permeated the air right before the tornado siren went off. As the sky broke with unbelievable sheets of rain, we all ran into the house and my grandmother told us to go to our rooms.

I hated that room. I hated that bed, and I hated those people, so I stomped up the stairs and I got on my knees and said, "God, if you are listening to me, please make all this nasty stuff stop and protect me and my little brother." Suddenly, a cross appeared over the door. I did not fully understand about God, but I knew He was the same God that saved my mother in the car accident.

From that day, no one touched me again, but the damage was already done. My experiences there had added fuel to the fire of my anger and bitterness. Not to mention the rejection, abandonment, torment and bad attitude I had against anyone in authority – not only with men, but with women as well.

I felt like my mom and dad threw me away and didn't care about me – especially if they were to find out about the horrific things that had been done to me.

After being at my grandmother's house for a month, I finally talked to my mom and begged her to let me come back home, but because of her emotional distance, she could not hear the brokenness in my voice.

Home Again

Five months later, my grandmother finally put us on a Greyhound bus back to Knoxville. My little brother and I were finally away from the house of pain.

I had a myriad of emotions and I just wanted to get home. Even though it was dysfunctional, it was the lesser of two evils. I wanted to run away, I wanted to fight, but one thing I didn't want to do was talk about my summer.

When my little brother and I pulled into the Greyhound Bus station, no one was there to meet us. I was good at this "taking care of" deal, so I got our bags and asked the ticket counter lady to please hold them at the counter because I needed to get my brother something to eat. He and I went across the street to the Blue Circle Cafe and got a hamburger, French fries and a cola. As we sat there and ate, I remember looking at the clock and seeing it was 4:10 p.m.

When my dad showed up at 5:30 p.m., I was glad and mad all at the same time. I know that sounds weird but I was glad because my dad was my common place of comfort even as I was mad that he wasn't there to protect me.

As we got in the car, he offered no apologies for being late. I was more focused on getting to my mom, but a surprise was waiting for us. It turned out we were going to live in the projects with our old great grandmother, my dad's twin brother, my cousin and my dad – all of us crammed into a two-bedroom apartment.

I just wanted to know where my mother was. But no one was interested in telling me.

I don't know if this is your story, or if you know someone who has experienced molestation or rape, but it is the most degrading and humiliating experience anyone will ever have. It takes away your identity, especially as a child.

They had no right to make me exchange my innocence for the indulgence of their perversion. I now carry the default of someone else's pain. The secret had become my cancer. It was spreading through my system slowly. I was made to take on adult feelings of seduction, and made to believe that I was only born to pleasure people who did this to little girls.

I didn't want anybody to see my body. I started dressing like a boy – wearing tube socks, gym shorts and baggy t-shirts. I also discovered I had the gift of speed, so I got into track and made that my place of safety and comfort.

I ran my heart out, to the point where my coach would ask me, "Ane, why do you run so hard?"

Why? Because I was mad as hell, that's why. And I didn't fully understand this at the time but I was releasing that pent-up anger.

As I carried that dark secret – being exposed to shotguns, house parties, jut joint perversion, etc., I couldn't tell the truth from a lie.

When we finally went back home to our mother, she could not understand why I was such an angry child. I was beaten, put on punishments and yelled and cursed at. But she could not comprehend that I was numb, because nothing could compare to the pain I experienced that summer from Hell. The more she would whoop me, the harder my inside became. As a child, I simply wanted to die.

I was miserable and my dreams of daddy were fading faster than the breath on a mirror. He was now in his other life with his new wife, and again I felt rejected.

Growing up, I did not hear the words "I love you" after my daddy left. My mother was not the affectionate type. She didn't like us all over her, so she really provided no place of comfort for us.

As a mid-teen, I was into sports, not boys, because I was living with this picture in the back of my mind of what had happened to me. This is reality for women who experience molestation and rape at a young age. They have commitment and trust issues, and they form their lives on the basis of fictional and dysfunctional emotions.

Some people may read about my life and sigh with relief that their own lives didn't have all the twists and turns mine has had. It's good to be able to tell yourself you've got it together and that your family was more like the Cleavers on "Leave It to Beaver" than like the one I'm describing.

If that's you, I applaud you, but you should still know something: when the hands stop clapping, we all spin from some sort of dysfunction in our homes. I always wondered why I had to deal with so much disarray in mine. It took a long time for the whole picture to come together, and for me to understand that I was born for someone else – some woman or young lady, or little girl or boy. I now have the opportunity to offer them a vision of hope and freedom.

This in no way excuses any bad decision I made. No one should ever do wrong and then try to justify it by saying it's so you can later teach someone else a lesson. But I have to deal from today forward with reality as it is.

One thing I learned through this process was that it takes 21 days to form a habit, but more than 20 years to break one. That habit may have started as a small baby snake, but it has now become a fire-breathing dragon. For me, it became my reality, a false sense of security in which I did not realize I was alienating and assassinating my own God-given character.

I deserved better than what my pain drove me into. I always knew within myself that there was something off about my choices. There were times when I would cry because no one was there for me to tell my "true self" to. So people ostracized me, talked about me and they dogged me, but never sought to hear my cry for help.

It was like a vicious cycle. I began to see traits of anger, rage and bitterness in my soul. I came out with the determination that no man would ever hurt me again. I had always been an affectionate child, but my affection was never seductive or perverted.

I began to give what I desired. I found myself becoming overbearing and overly loyal, and trying to be a rescuer. I lived my life yearning for love from my mother, from my dad, from anybody that could make me feel safe.

One year, I remember saving money to buy my mama a gift for her birthday. I did not use my lunch money for food because I wanted to make my mother smile. I vividly recall getting off of the bus and walking into a small jewelry store. I entered and saw this beautiful rose necklace on a gold chain. My eyes stretched so wide because I wanted to get that for my mom. Then the "slinky" bracelets came out, and I wanted to get my mom one of those bracelets too!

I felt like a kid who won a ticket to tour Willy Wonka's Chocolate Factory! I was so excited about that necklace. It was $5.00, and the bracelet was $2.00. That's just a few gallons of gas today but back then it was a lot of money, especially for a kid.

I saved my $7.00 and anxiously sat on the bus. The date

was November 30, 1978, and I was going to get my mother's jewelry. The bus could not get to the end of Washington Avenue quickly enough. I was on the edge of my seat, hoping that no one came into that store and purchased the necklace with the beautiful red rose on it.

I pulled the strap on the bus and stood at the top of the steps waiting for the bus to stop. As it did, and the door opened, I jumped off the steps and ran a block to the corner where the jewelry store was. I ran in and there it was – that beautiful gold chain with the red rose at the end. I counted out seven one-dollar bills. I remember he did not charge me tax, because I told the man I was buying it for my mom's birthday.

I ran home, rushed into my room and hid the gift under my bed. I could hardly sleep I had so much anticipation of the smile that would fill my mother's face. I kept looking at it. I tried it on, all the while singing "God Bless the Child" by Billie Holiday.

On my mother's birthday, I ran into the room and yelled, "HAPPY BIRTHDAY MAMA!"

I pulled the pretty white box from behind my back and said, "Look, Mama, look!" I gave her the bracelet first, and then the finale of the beautiful gold chain with the pretty red rose on the end.

She looked at it and said to me, "I don't like it."

I was devastated. My inside was void. I was so stunned that I just stood there. She said, "Hurry up, I can't be late to work!"

So here I was again, rejected and abandoned, such a familiar place for me. Even writing this today, in this very quiet, still moment, it opens up old wounds and brings on new tears.

I cried all the way to school. As she dropped me off at Maynard Elementary School, I said, "I love you, mama."

And she pulled away. I was crushed! All day in school, I thought about the necklace. It was still beautiful to me. I went home that day after school and found the necklace in my mom's Chester drawer. I left it there. She never wore it or the bracelet.

Why did I share that story? Because this was another root in my life, and from that day I began to absolutely hate red roses. I made it very clear to all of my friends and family that I hated red roses. It wasn't until my girlfriend from Dothan, Alabama, gave me a dozen red roses on March 25, 2011, that the Lord healed that wound in my life. I missed the ability to enjoy the beauty that I beheld that day in that rose. I deprived lovers, family and friends from expressing their affection to me by buying me red roses.

I had to pray and ask God to heal my broken life. Healing is definitely a process, but it feels so good to finally appreciate not only the beauty of a red rose but the person who thought enough of me to purchase them. To smell their brilliance as their petals unfold, to feel their allure of expression and exclusive velvety texture.

I share all of this with you so you can find your root, or roots, that have been choking the life out of your progression to freedom.

There are three areas that shape our lives:
1. Our families
2. Our environment
3. Our teachers

I wrote this chapter in order to create a picture and a platform that can help get to the root of what makes us choose and think the way we do.

Sure, we're naturally wired differently because that's the way God created us. But much of how we think and behave is the result of when we've been faced with harsh challenges, circumstances beyond our control and people that have a monumental effect on our psychological health. That's how we get stuck in the same old cycles.

I want to encourage you to use this book as your personal journal. Make notes. Jot things down as they come to memory. I'm a big believer in the idea that when you write things down, it's therapeutic and it makes you feel better.

This isn't just another self-help book. It's the beginning of your healing.

Final Thoughts

I was broken and angry; bitter by life's misuse of my soul
Mad, wanting people to pay…the hatred in me was on a roll
Down on the inside of my dainty lil cry…I wanted to be a girl, so why can't I
Please, someone rescue me from the world of darkness and shame
Will anyone heal me so I can finally know my name?
Then years of obscurity shape my path and form my views
I dare not lay down the best of me and allow people to give me rules
I need to break out of this glass so that I can be free
To do what I want to do and be who I want to be
How can I stride with so much pain and abuse?
I can't…so I had to shake my soul loose
So before you judge my path to success
Check your own background
and you will find we all have journeyed through mess
Think about it before you pull the trigger and shoot
I am cutting and releasing all my roots
If no one celebrates my coming out party, I will in deed
I will scream from the rooftop and from the valley low,
I am free, thank God, I am FREE in me…
Finally

"There comes a point when you either embrace who and what you are, or condemn yourself to be miserable all your days. Other people will try to make you miserable; don't help them by doing the job yourself."

— Laurell K. Hamilton

Chapter Two

The Spot

"If you don't know yourself, you will always make choices from the broken person within you. Our lives are a sum total of the choices we have made." – Wayne Dyer

I used to tell myself that I am a risk taker – not knowing that most times they were not risks but were acts of unsettled apprehensions. I would rationalize my choices by saying to myself that I was a good judge of character. But how could I make those types of decisions when I could not even judge my own inner mayhem?

There would be times when I would choose relationships from the place in me where there was no drama, but there was no peace either. I cannot explain to you the times that I felt sure of myself and my choices only to end up desolate and regretful of the thing that I allowed to be my demise.

I have wasted so much time on people who were not worthy of my energy or effort. I had to acknowledge that there was a spot in me that needed to be filled. I was impatient with God and with my process to becoming more in sync and unity with me.

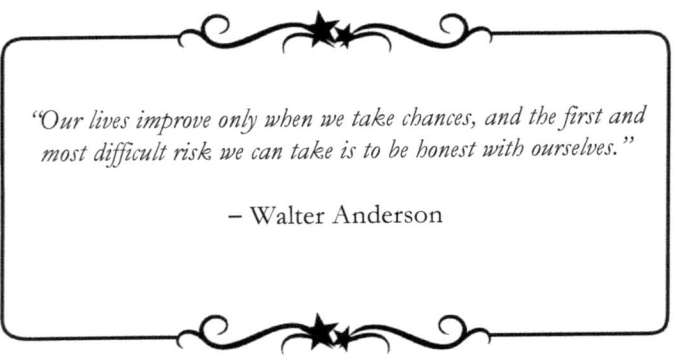

"Our lives improve only when we take chances, and the first and most difficult risk we can take is to be honest with ourselves."

– Walter Anderson

We can be our own fool, and I was.

I thought I was a wise woman, full of God and experience, until I met the woman within me that asked the question: "When are you going to allow me to live?"

I did not understand this question that kept resonating in my soul. That place in me as a woman that refused to die but was starving to live. To the outside world, I had become this powerful, progressive person. Inside I felt powerless. I became aware of the fact that I had created a world in which I could no longer breathe. I was shy of life and absent of being. I was my own god in that I felt as if life had taught me to be responsible for my actions and choices. My attitude was, "I got this, I am good, life could be worse." I found myself attracting the kinds of men I never should have been involved with. So once again, I was pouring into people who yielded me absolutely no return.

I was dealing with things I never should have involved

myself with when I thought that season of my life was over. I did not want to be the "strong woman" in the relationship. I had put away the superwoman costume and was now living for my man. I said, "Now that I have a strong man, I can begin the next path of life for myself and with him." I felt like God and life had rewarded me only to end up relationally depleted. I had resurrected the old woman on the inside that deliverance had buried.

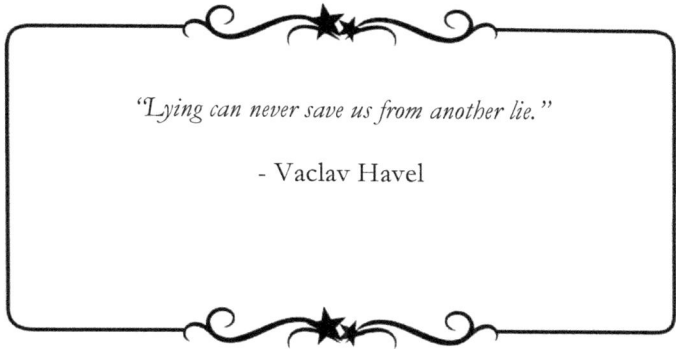

"Lying can never save us from another lie."

- Vaclav Havel

During the course of this relationship I told many lies to myself to create safety when in reality I felt like I was in a war zone. What a bitter pill it is to swallow when you think you can exhale with relief but in truth you are gripped with fear. One day, I looked around and was shocked by where I found myself on the journey to self-improvement.

I was moving but going nowhere. I was finding myself – angry again, bitter again, frustrated like hell again – wanting to separate from this beast that I had felt so compatible with before.

Then it hit me: I wasn't angry with him, my anger was with myself! I was disappointed in my values, age was my measure of grace, I thought, until I felt together but separated, in a relationship but alone, communicating but not talking. I was embarrassed, but could not feel pity for my choices. I had enough strength to know that I could not succumb to the power of self-inflicted drama but I needed God to fix this.

I was becoming a woman who dreamed but didn't produce. I began to fight with the man who before I had been so adamant God had sent to me. I felt like a failure to myself and my children. My life became consumed with the problems we were having, and for months I asked, "How can I free myself?"

I wanted help, but I was not praying for it. I did not have any desire for God to help me. I wanted out of the situation physically, so I checked out mentally. I was done, absent and non-caring.

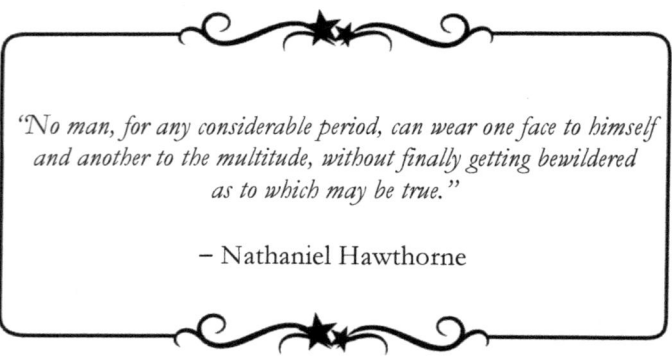

"No man, for any considerable period, can wear one face to himself and another to the multitude, without finally getting bewildered as to which may be true."

– Nathaniel Hawthorne

Who can you talk to when so many other people see you as the source of support and encouragement? To whom can you admit your own vulnerability?

I've found that to be an especially perplexing question in dealing with relationships. The picture people see may look perfect, but when the reality is that it's an effort to hold hands or to crack a genuine smile, you realize that you may be doing what you think is morally correct to do – but you're not really doing what's in your heart.

After enough of that, I needed an answer from no one but God to this question: From what spot inside myself was I choosing these relationships? Clearly I was responding to a need I felt to be connected to someone, and to enjoy the ambiance of love. What I was definitely not doing was waiting on God's choice for me. I wasn't waiting for the man God had picked out as truly compatible with me, as truly intertwined in the spirit, as joined together in the soul. I was strictly following my surface impulses, and where was that getting me?

I'll tell you where. It got me to a place where I looked around at all the powerful women I knew in my life, and I saw that they had the sternness in their hearts to stay in their marriages or relationships. And they all seemed to have beautiful reasons for the choices they made. But not me. Not Ane. I was always the one who could never seem to resolve a situation any other way than moving on alone.

And to be honest, I had become so arrogant in my own will, I didn't even know how to fight for a relationship that was worth it. I saw people who were able to miss someone who was in the very same house with them. Who could hurt over a relationship just because it meant so much to them. I tried to let myself want that, but I didn't know how. Every instinct I had told me that it was weakness to feel that way. To me, walking away was the only way to show strength.

Contemplating fears from and of the unknown, I found myself in the middle of nowhere, wanting to go somewhere different but having no clue where that might be.

And now I find myself once again at a pivotal moment in my life, but this time I know better than to point the finger at anyone but myself. I have to challenge myself: What is this spot in me that causes me to choose relationships like this? And why are people more shocked by honesty than by deceit?

One thing I know from conversations with God and with myself – I don't know how much you pray but you need to know this: God gives everyone the power of choice. Taking my life back and maintaining it was vital to my rebirth – I had to live and complete my purpose.

Thomas Jefferson said something that blew my mind: "It is of great importance to set a resolution, not to be shaken, never to tell an untruth. There is no vice so mean, so pitiful, so contemptible; and he who permits himself to tell a lie once finds it much easier to do it a second and a third time, till at length it becomes habitual; he tells lies without attending to it, and truths without the world's believing him. This falsehood of the tongue leads to that of the heart and in time depraves all its good dispositions."

This is exactly where I found myself: repeatedly contradicting my own values and standards of being a woman. I sought counseling because I could not discuss this issue with my best friend or my circle of sisters.

I needed an unbiased opinion. I did not need another person to say, "Girl, I got you."

There comes a point in your life when you re-evaluate and start making healthy choices. But that will only happen when you release a different kind of woman from inside of you.

This may be a woman who you have never really known. She understands it is better to let God make her choices instead of continuing to choose from that spot that keeps reaching out to those who can't or won't edify her, and don't afford her the opportunity to heal within herself. You know those men, and the woman you need to bring out won't choose to let them define her life or her priorities. They are her opposite.

Instead, she'll choose to fight for herself before she fights for his survival – not out of selfishness but simply out of the realization that she can't help anyone if she is always broken herself.

I spent too much time in that cycle, and it wasn't only manifested in my relationships with men. It also characterized the way I approached motherhood. I was using my own children as my place of survival, and that made them victims of my own unsuited personhood. I did them no good by remaining in such an unsettled state and telling myself it was fine as long as I took care of them.

So whether in my marriage or my role as a mother, I was performing a role rather than loving the life I was living and the people around me. Even church seemed like a role I was playing, and it was a lot of work to play that role. Blahhhhhhhhhhhhhhh.

I got to the point where I didn't want to be the answer for anyone, and I was fed up with people pulling on me for answers when inside I was fainting.

One day I was downstairs preparing breakfast for my children and my son Moo said, "Mom, why are grown people afraid to confront who they really are?"

I told him it was because it hurts too much. His response to that was it is better to live free. I am telling you – that hit me in my gut. Did I want to get back in the game or live my life wondering, "Where do I go from here?"

So now, after recognizing that I was not really living, I had to take a deep breath and again deal with the health of my being. I was determined to stop making dumb choices. Relationships should always be give and take; love and war; mistakes and growth. It is being understood and learning; sowing and reaping; being best friends and lovers. It is being the one who captivates my heart in a crowded room; it is giving your partner the space to fail but never letting them feel defeated. It is dreaming and daydreaming; it is the working of two lives that come together – not to crash and burn but sharpen and push and support.

It was time to stop lying to myself – that is not what I had, and that was not what I offered. But was there too much emotional damage to repair? Were the walls of trust so damaged that there was nothing to build on or for? Was there so much resentment that love was just a has-been opportunity? Was it love or was it the fear of being alone? Should I walk away or deal with it honestly?

Epictetus said, "The greater the difficulty, the more glory in surmounting it. Skillful pilots gain their reputation from storms and tempests."

I loved that quote and would repeat it over and over because I was striving to make it so. But here's the question: Was I strong enough to survive the tempest? My inner woman was tired of storms.

The fact is, I had children now, and they are mature enough to know that my choices affect them. We as parents sometimes make selfish decisions, not understanding that these little people have a heart as well. They have emotions and fears.

I had to strategically heal me and them at the same time, because even with all the covering and protecting and smiling through the pain and the drama, children detect atmospheres in a home. In addition to my older daughter, I was also raising two younger boys. So I needed to recognize that I was raising my babies to be someone's husband and father. What lessons was I allowing them to learn from me? What was I showing my daughter, being in this dysfunctional relationship? I had to pull it together, take my power back and shift from being a victim.

My sisters, what's so true is that pain never lies and healing never hurts. These two work simultaneously but we as people do not embrace them. We oftentimes tie it to the worst of the process than the acceptable plan of reconciliation to truth.

We internally become territorial concerning the wrong parts of our discovery. We portray damaging pictures of lies and call it protecting. By all means, protect your life, but don't believe the lies you have painted and call it a portrait. Over the course of time it will not stand, the real you will fight to live.

I chose to become who God had created me to be, and to value in my life the part I had fought so hard to gain. I had compromised to be in a relationship. I adapted to be his vision, believing and supporting his life but maintaining the woman who I lived to enjoy.

I was not fearful of living for me again. I embraced the fact that life is a difficult, unpredictable climb but the view is breathtaking! It was my perception of the view that changed my outlook. I had taken a backseat to push something I had lost a connection to and a passion for, but I trained myself to be a puppet master.

I would be wiser, if only due to the fact that people were watching my every move, and I realized that my choices wouldn't just impact me but they would impact the people who call me friend, sister and mentor.

Had I become what I counseled, avoided what I forewarned others about – preaching to so many sisters about getting into the wrong relationships, reminding them that they were too valuable to settle – I would have been more than just the ray of hope and sunshine to others that was mandated by the transparency of my journey. I might have been real and whole inside. Instead, I wanted to vomit at the advice I gave others because I could not embrace it for myself.

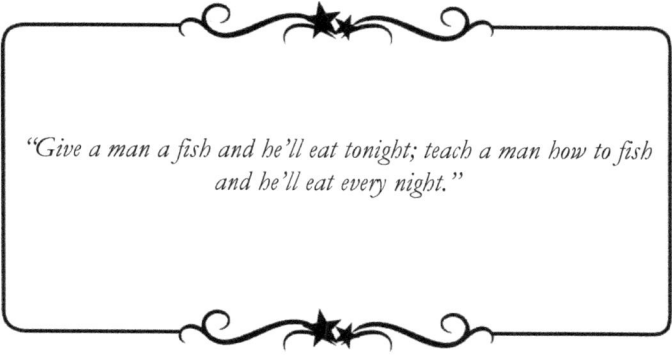

"Give a man a fish and he'll eat tonight; teach a man how to fish and he'll eat every night."

My relationship choices could never keep me fulfilled and satisfied over the long term. They were only giving me what I felt I needed in a moment, and only sometimes, and never on any sort of sustained basis.

I was like that man who was given the fish. It wasn't what I needed. I wanted to eat every night, not starting and stopping, hitting and missing – always feeling unsure. And through that experience, God showed me: If I insisted on making the choices, then I would have to deal with the consequences. But if I left the choice to God and was willing to be obedient to His choices, then the consequences would be left to Him.

When you realize that, your entire perspective changes about how you experience the day-to-day realities of a relationship. You don't cut and run in the dark moments because you understand that even they are better living with than without, and you know you will always weather them better as part of the team God made you to be part of.

With the right person, this is easy to understand. You don't fear staying. You don't feel consternation over the work it takes to keep the love and relationship healthy. You do all this happily because, with the person God picked out for you, it's clearly worth it.

Accepting fish wasn't going to get me to this. I started to realize that I needed to find the fisherman, and that meant I had to stop pushing the issue according to my own will and trust God to bring him to me.

Stop trying to change the man to fit into your world and just wait to learn how to fish. It is a better path.

Every woman needs to feel safe in the confinements of her world. It's something you create for yourself and it should be provided by your man. You have to be comfortable enough in your own skin to trust your man when he is sent to you, regardless of who has hurt you.

Choose to turn that hurt into a measuring stick to use for future decisions. Lesson learned: Never offer what you haven't been healed of. I knew something had died in me because I stopped being who I was. I stopped writing – I had writer's block. I felt destitute, absent of progression.

You cannot be afraid to remove yourself or put a demand on the relationship to change. Demand doesn't mean being forceful against your mate's life. It is realizing you either made a mistake or you deserve more, and until you realize that you are worth more than what you have allowed yourself to settle for you will always be an empty dreamer.

Now, I had to come to this finality: Me minus you creates a new beginning, but me minus God is a devastation.

I used to look in the mirror of my soul and ask myself this great Disney slogan: "Mirror mirror on the wall, who's the fairest of them all?"

At this junction of my life I had matured from the Disney mirror. Now I am seeing the reflection in a much broader view.

I could no longer hold it in my hand. It was not controllable. This relationship was reflecting in the mirror what I saw in myself, and the years were slowly revealing the unhealthiness of my decision. The question kept coming up: How do I fix it? But I couldn't because I had not fixed myself.

See, the state of consciousness that I had was to always fix everything and everybody, but I was denying that I still needed to fix that spot in me so I could heal. I could no longer put emphasis on my outward image. I had to really dig deep and say to myself, "You are not the same woman. You have changed and have turned into this woman who has allowed herself to be stopped from living."

I finally realized that I am not responsible for something that I no longer could pour into or support. I couldn't feel guilty for wanting to take care of myself. I had to believe again that I am simply a woman – amazing, gifted, sexual, intimate – a woman of wealth, power and blessings. I had to rediscover my position in life that God had afforded me. I had to own that I may have issues, but I am far from being finished.

I began to strip away every negative force that I had empowered through my loneliness and anger. I had to believe that I am okay (with a little crazy on the side!)
YES! YES! YES! The most important thing is that I make it to a healthy place within me.

I was finally okay with admitting that I just needed

more. I was fine with questioning my decisions, (Did I make a mistake?) and even if I didn't I could now bring myself to the place of being able to not feel guilty.

If I stayed in that unhealthy emotion I would always find myself questioning and judging the power of my choices. I decided to deactivate that place in me that was ruling my ability to choose things and people who were not healthy for me. I heard someone say, "You will never change what you tolerate." So stop being tolerant of what you know is not good for your life!

Let me say this: Making a healthy choice doesn't always require you to leave an individual. Sometimes it just means putting your foot down to live a better life or asking your partner to rise to the challenge of growing together in a healthy relationship. You grow together or your choice will cause you to grow apart.

Even in making that choice, trust me: Your change will expose the true heart of the one you are in a relationship with. Also, you making better choices does not mean that your partner is a bad person – they simply may no longer be profitable to your life.

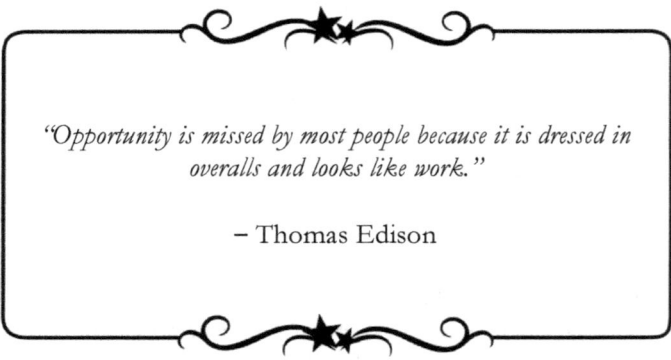

"Opportunity is missed by most people because it is dressed in overalls and looks like work."

– Thomas Edison

Am I saying if you are married just go get a divorce? No way! I'm saying if you are married then there needs to be some sort of communication and room for both partners to be better and live healthy – together.

Lesson learned: Never get into a relationship holding on to the pain of your last one. Use it as wisdom, not as a fighting tactic.

Lesson still learning: I have to be more valuable to myself before I can be a value to a man. I am beautiful, yes, but I am even more beautiful as a tapped source of resolution.

So sisters, in the course of taking back my life and living, I learned that there are still places within ourselves that require attention, but they are great places of self-discovery. You are too special and unique to be wasted.

Chapter Three

Secrets Are Not Sassy

Wow. It is amazing that when this chapter came to me I was wondering how I would comprise all the years of my life that to me were represented as "special", not realizing that they were not special, they were simply rules with understanding.

You may ask, "What does 'rules with understanding' mean?" I will tell you. Rules with understanding boils down to this conversation:

"Listen, you know that I love you. You and I share a special bond that I have never had before with any other woman but right now is not the time for us to be open with our relationship, so let's create our own little world just for you and me."

It's just you and me. Just the two of us! I oftentimes think of a theme song to undergird an experience in my life and what better song than "Secret Lovers"? I recalled my life and tried to figure out what made me lower myself to become a man's secret?

I am of the essence that no one can make you do anything – you choose to be a partner in any relationship, be it willingly, ignorantly or knowingly.

My mother conceived me when she was a teenager – in the '60s, not having the best life at home, in high school and hiding that she was pregnant. What an embarrassment it had to be for her (bless her!), so even in the beginning of my life I was hidden, until I began to grow (that's another message within itself.) Then growing up, as you read in previous chapters, I had to hide the molestation as I went into my first experience of having a relationship with a married man.

Now, I was a new convert to the faith, and on top of that I was saved in a "Holiness Church." What an experience that was, let me tell you! I was a 19-year-old single mother of a beautiful little boy who was the joy of my life. That baby was my life and I held him close. He was my priority and I knew that I had to protect and take care of him but I was so confused about the direction of my life at that time – on welfare and living in subsidized housing.

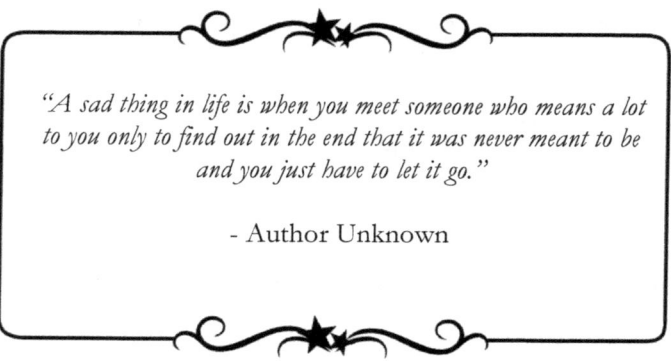

"A sad thing in life is when you meet someone who means a lot to you only to find out in the end that it was never meant to be and you just have to let it go."

- Author Unknown

I wanted so much for my life to be different. Struggling with where I was and the demands that the holiness church put on me, and yet still wanting to be a girl, a teen, a young lady, and wrestling with the feeling of wanting to fit in somewhere. Even on the system I was so determined to be a successful woman. I was now in the church, riding the church van faithfully because I wanted to learn about this Jesus stuff.

My experience was pleasant but those people were weird. They jumped and ran, they hollered and spoke in a language that sounded like baby babble, and I was totally unfamiliar with the "church world" and how it operated, but all I knew was that the people who were in the church said that church faithfulness was needed to stay free! I was not all the way ignorant to the church – my grandmother, Mother Wheelwright, was a praying woman and loved the Lord with all her heart.

As a child I went to church but didn't have much regard for it. I enjoyed when the older mothers would come over to my grandmother's house and would have "Prayer Circles". The power of God that was in her home was unbelievable! Those were some praying and precious women.

As I grew up, I was given to, and befriended by, a deacon at the church who was an older gentleman. He showed a special care for me and my son, and would make sure that we had what we needed – like medicine when my son was sick, and money in my pocket between checks. I thought, "Wow, this man is really nice!"

I realized he was attracted to me, and I wasn't completely comfortable with it. At the same time, the father of my son – with whom I was in a relationship – was not treating me well.

Soon I became this man's confidante at 19, which I was certainly not ready for. And it didn't take long from this point for me to become the church's Jezebel. I'd never been treated so nicely, and although I knew it was wrong to be involved with a married man – I had a strong conviction about that – my naiveté and vulnerability got the best of me. I tried to deal with it by confiding in a woman in the church that I believed I could trust. That was a mistake.

So as the situation spiraled and my reputation got worse, I faced the absurd prospect of moving in with him and his wife. I know that sounds crazy, but I had lost my apartment and I was not on good terms with my mother. So they took me in. But I realized quickly that it was a bad situation, and to make things even more absurd, his mother also lived there!

All the while, I encouraged this man to think of me as the person he could talk to about his marital issues, which was a huge mistake. What did I know about it? And no man should ever be talking to another woman about his marital issues anyway, but that was beyond my understanding at that point. I should not have been carrying the burden of a married man's problems, and I was not equipped to do so.

The whole situation made no sense, and as the 19-year-old confidante of a church leader, I was completely denying myself the chance to live like a 19-year-old. When the relationship finally did turn sexual, it was surreal. Here I was attending this man's church and I had a relationship with his family, yet I had this secret I had to protect. Many times I wanted to just back away from the whole thing but he pleaded with me to stay because he would have no one else to confide in if I left.

I was terribly conflicted. My son noticed changes in my behavior. My pastor – who knew about the affair – said he would protect me. He tried to bring the relationship to an end, and I knew that was what needed to happen, but I didn't know how to do it. Soon I was put out of the church. My reputation in tatters, I started drinking and partying, and it wasn't long before I became involved with a drug dealer.

The drug dealer, of course, represented an entirely different kind of appeal. He was something new, and I was ready to embrace the money, the cars and the rest of the lifestyle. It was still spiritual suicide but it took a different form and it seemed fresh to me. The flash of the lifestyle made it a little easier for me to deny I was destroying my own potential – that I was working against the anointing

God had placed on my life.

And because people feared him, they looked out for me too, and I was able to mistake that for real respect. But I was nowhere on the realization of my own dreams. If you want to do that, you have to not only recognize what God is trying to do in your life but you have to chase after it with tenacity. Slumming with a drug dealer and glomming onto the fake esteem he gets from his crew is not the way to do that. It's what you do when your own self-esteem is in the toilet and you can't bring yourself to work toward anything of real value.

And that's where I was.

Now, I never tried drugs myself, but this man made lots of money dealing and I got caught up in the lifestyle. I also got pregnant inside of six months.

Not wanting the drug dealer to know he was the father of my child, I tried to convince the deacon the child was his. That was a tough sell because he knew himself to be sterile, but I tried to sell the idea that God had performed a miracle!

He didn't buy it. Finally, I had to tell the truth. But it was too late to save his marriage. He moved out and filed for divorce. Now what was I supposed to do? I tried to tell myself I could handle the burden of being with him, but at my age there was no way I was ready for it. I would leave him only to come back to him, as he would constantly make me feel like I was doing him wrong not to stand by his side. He kept telling me that everything he was doing was "for us."

One friend encouraged me to swallow castor oil in order to kill the baby. I was so scared about the situation that I actually tried it. I drank two bottles. Thank God, it didn't work. There was also a local doctor who was known to give out pills to women who didn't want to have their babies. I got my hands on some of those too. I took the whole bottle. It didn't even cause any bleeding, and the baby just kept holding on.

Next I thought that starving myself might end the

pregnancy. I didn't eat for three days. But during this period I heard a voice in my spirit – and I knew it was God's voice – telling me that He had plans for this child. I needed to change my attitude and focus on the life that was growing inside me.

Bre-Onna Dayon was born September 17, 1989. She had beautiful brown eyes and I was determined not to subject her to the type of life I'd been living myself. I believed I was purposed to make her the queen of the world.

Returning to the church from which we had just been put out was not the best first move toward making that happen, unfortunately. I'll keep people's names to myself for a variety of reasons, but many blamed me not just for what I'd personally been involved with, but for exposing a side of life there that they would have preferred stay hidden.

In the midst of all this, I raised my daughter in the guilt of my shame, and spoiled her with lavish things because of my regrets. When her drug-dealer dad got out of jail, he wanted to see her. When he looked at her, he cried and talked about how much he loved her. But he didn't see her again until her ninth birthday. In the meantime, I was married to the deacon and living a lie. I started to have an affair with a childhood friend, in addition to trying to make something of my life by going to college – since partying wasn't bringing me any fulfillment.

Before you decide to live in that secret realize it will affect your kids, not just you.

I made the choice to leave my marriage. It was not in my children's best interests to live in this world of what you might call true lies. And what, exactly, does it mean to live a true lie? In this case, for me, it meant that I was keeping his vulnerability hidden from the world. I became his place of detoxification – his safe place. But once again, I was merely a secret lover. I learned to function in the role of his play wife, doing what his wife wouldn't do at home.

You get to play the role. You feel special and cute and you build your world around this man. I found this very natural, because I know how to be romantic – how to cater to a man. I could shop for him, pay attention to the condition of his clothing. I pay attention to style, so I could give him all kind of ideas for how to make a better him.

And I could do a lot more, too. I love sports, so I could experience that with him. I could write him poems. I could cook his favorite meals and challenge his intellect. I could make him feel like he was my priority, and he would respond to that.

But I was still a secret. It all happened behind closed doors. There could never be open affection. We could establish that "we wish" we could be together, but we never really could be. Eventually I would also have to be told it's "not time yet," or reminded, "you know my situation." You might become his traveling wife – always being sure to go wherever he goes when he leaves town, since that's the perfect opportunity for you and him to be together. But you're also lying to the people in your life about what you're really doing.

And eventually an argument was inevitable, because he's enjoying all of you, but you're not enjoying all of him. He's your man, but he still belongs to another woman. You're sexually married but really single.

That's an especially difficult trap for me, because I know how to treat a man. I am attentive. I take care of his needs. And whether it's a 90-minute massage he needs, an upgrade in his style, or an uplifting text at just the right moment – I know how to make sure he gets it. It's no wonder married men gravitate toward me. And I don't mean to suggest it's all an act. I really do enjoy seeing the smiles on their faces, and feeling as though I made a difference.

That's part of what gets me in trouble, of course. I would pour my soul into these relationships, and there were little rewards along the way, but ultimately I was still investing everything I had into something that was not quite mine, not quite real, and never truly permanent. No matter what I gave him, he wasn't going to give me back the same thing because I wasn't really his.

And of course, it could never really come out in the open. And eventually, the little rewards would be outweighed by the burden you were never really going to get the commitment you'd want after pouring yourself into another person like that. Your emotional investment now leaves you empty, and that affects everything about your life. It affects your performance at work. It affects your finances. It affects your relationships with other women. You know your heart shouldn't be so tied to this, but you're so deep into it, it's nearly impossible to pull away.

Most people who get into secret relationships are vulnerable and broken. They have battered hearts and low self-esteem. They're searching for acceptance. That was me. Some elements of it – the cars, the money, the jewelry, the trips – were nice for a while. But they were never worth the embarrassment to me, to my children and to my family.

And the truth is that my "secret" was never really secret. Maybe some of the details were, but my emotions and my damaged heart weren't hidden from anyone.

After a while, you don't even realize it but you have become a weeping willow tree. Its beauty has a falling canopy. It has a dramatic appearance, perfect for those looking for a quick way of adding character and value to your property. It has the ability to absorb standing water. And although willows are found near living waters, it has the ability to grow just about anywhere, even demonstrating some tolerance in droughts. A weeping willow can be very adaptable to all kinds of soils and growing conditions. You will enjoy this tree as the first harbinger in the spring when its leaves appear before a lot of other trees – and it will be the last to shed its leaves in the fall. This tree is known for its grace, distinctiveness and beauty.

That's a pretty good representation of a woman caught in a secret relationship with a married man. The man loves a strong, powerful, intellectual, graceful, beautiful and emotionally stable woman. He loves it when he can gloat that his woman has it all together. You are like this willow tree. You're adaptable. You can flow with sudden changes in your plans with him, since you always realize the family and his wife are going to come first, even if he is unhappy.

By the way, this can happen in a relationship with a single man too. Just because he's not cheating on a wife doesn't necessarily mean he is willing to honor you and show you off. If you're getting that kind of treatment from a man, you should ask yourself why. Why are you good enough to whisper to but not to be shown off? You deserve better than that, and there is someone God has for you who will happily honor you in that way.

If a man won't treat you with that kind of respect, don't accept it from him just because he is single! Eventually you won't be willing to accept it anymore, and you'll start yelling. You'll let him know you've had it with this #@(*!

And you know what? As soon as you become hysterical, that's when you become historical. Maybe you would have been better off not to let yourself become the secret woman in the first place.

I realize there are some who think it's not only acceptable, but actually desirable, to be in a relationship with lots of sex and goodies, but with no real emotional commitment. They say, hey, we're all grownups and it's our choice. But there's a difference between exercising the discretion that's yours as an adult and walking in real wisdom. Too often we make choices based on how we feel right now, rather than on what we should know will be the consequences of those choices.

And here's an angle you may not have considered when it comes to getting involved with a married man: Why, sisters, do you want to stand in the way of his making it with his mate? If you love him as you claim, why complicate that? Because you're in subjection to a man who cannot cover you wholeheartedly. He can't protect you, take care of you, look after you or make decisions that concern your life. You know how you want him to feel the dynamic of your connection with him when you and he are making love? That's never going to happen in the way you want because he's not wholly yours.

These are some of the reasons God forbids adultery. He knows what it leads to. This man is trying to love you with his skill, but he can never make a covenant with you before God. It's his marriage that God wants to honor, and the relationship you're having with him will never be acceptable in God's eyes. This is why it causes the mess it does. It can never be healthy, for you or for anyone else it touches.

This is why you need to take back your life and make choices that lead to healthy situations – not to situations that need to keep to secret shadows. And if you know someone who is in a situation like this, encourage her to do the same. I realized this one day as I was praying, asking God to help me. I was looking out the window and the rain was falling. I could not see in the darkness, with the storm gathering and lightning occasionally flashing across the sky. It was quiet in my room and tears were rolling down my face. I felt abandoned by my own belief system, because of course I knew this was wrong.

I felt like I was enveloped in inner turmoil – alone and scared. I could not believe my shell was open, such that I was now tied emotionally to someone I could not even talk to. I could not open up and detoxify to him because he was not available. I realized my insides felt like the weather. My tears were the rain; the clouds were my judgment. The thunder represented my spirit not being at peace, and the lightning represented the danger of my bitterness now breaking away, turning me into a woman who would become hard and protective.

I had to go through all this alone. I could not tell anyone because I felt the shame of it myself. If this is you, I survived to be your answer. I took the hit for you. And you need to understand: Just because you found yourself in this type of situation does not mean that you are a bad person or that he is a bad person. This is a clear and true image of two broken people trying to rescue what they cannot heal. Be free and heal your life.

I did!

Private Relationships

The private relationship is a variation on the secret one. Private relationships consist of you and him and your friends. Everyone knows about him in your world but no one knows about you in his world. It's not necessarily because he's married. He may or may not be, but he's got some reason he doesn't want to identify in his world as being in a relationship with you.

He might tell you he's "working through something" (a divorce, a job situation, whatever) and that he needs you to understand and be patient while he keeps it on the "down low" for a period of time.

One of my worst experiences here involved a man who told me we had to keep it on the down low for three months or so because he was going through a divorce. It seemed like something I could handle, and we talked on the phone constantly. We seemed to have a great relationship. And that's when I decided I wanted to surprise him by flying to his location. This was when the red flags started popping up.

He did pick me up, but 30 minutes late, informing me, "I'll explain later."

That was a sign.

Next, he asked me if I was hungry. Yes! I was! So he said he would pick me up at 9 p.m. to go and eat, which would have sounded great if not for the fact that it was 2:30 p.m. at the time. I was expected to sit around the hotel the entire day while he did whatever he needed to do, and only then could I see him.

We ate late. We never went out anywhere. I never met his family. And then I got dropped off at the airport without so much as an escort into the terminal. I walked to my gate, sat down and began to journal. It started like this: "What a private three days this was, one of the dumbest things a girl could have ever done. Wake up Ane, the proof is written on the wall. You are not the only one that is in a relationship with this man."

I struggled with the fact that he seemed adamant about me, and gave every indication that he really liked me. But I couldn't deny what I was seeing. This was never going to go any farther than this. I had to leave it alone. It was painful because I was really into this guy, and he struck me as a lonely gentleman. But while my world had embraced him, I was never going to receive that embrace back from him.

He wouldn't let it happen.

Still, I didn't let it go that easily. I started questioning him when he didn't answer his phone, which only aggravated him. He didn't think he owed me any explanation beyond, "I told you my situation!"

Yes, he had. And while I interpreted the situation as a relationship, he only saw it as friendship with maybe the possibility of something more.

I probably should have just let it go at that point, but I wanted to know the truth. So I hired a private investigator to break into his phone – using password hints I was able to provide. Eventually the P.I. got in and we were able to listen to message after message from other women.

How had I not seen this? Why had I ignored the signs? The conversations I had with him seemed to suggest a real bond between us, but just because we shared a lot doesn't mean he was really making a commitment to me. Oh, by the way, he was already divorced. He was just using that situation as an excuse to keep within the limits of the game. Since he knew I wasn't interested in dating any more married men, pretending he wasn't divorced yet gave him a checkmate on my process.

I had revealed that about myself, but I didn't really know the hand he was playing with.

Why had all this happened? I talked to a male friend and he explained it from a man's perspective: "You scared him when you started asking questions. You pulled a move he was not expecting, and so in order for him not to commit he backed away, because everything about you says commitment and settlement, you were simply not willing to live his lie."

What really messed me up was when he said, "Ane, you are the woman all men desire! You got it!"

I was floored because I was sure he meant what he said. So now I am dealing with having "got it." Great. Got what? And if I did, then why was I single?

At this time in my life, I was not lonely. My life was flowing. It was good and being a single mom was working for me. So why was I attracting different men, but with the same spirit, the same traits, and same attributes?

Then it hit me: It wasn't them, it was what I was willing to accept. When you choose from your painful place, you reap unhealthiness.

I am not so oblivious as to think there is a perfect person out there. But I do know that when God brings you your mate, even in difficulty your love does not fade. The two of you work together to build a happy and strong relationship, and the goal is attainable because God ordained it.

And I can't control who God brings to me, or what he's like, but I can control who I am. So I started to peel the onion back on myself and analyze who I really was – and why I reacted to men in the way that I did. One thing I realized is that I didn't handle suspicions toward men very well. It doesn't do you any good to charge at them, or to interrogate them with complex questions. They don't react well to that. They'll retreat, or they'll find a way out of the conversation.

You need to confront the situation calmly, when you can make him comfortable enough to sit down to talk.

But also recognize: These problems are inherent to

private-only conversations, and because there is so much danger it's only a matter of time before rage influences you and the way you're handling things.

I have no one to blame but myself for any of this, of course. I made all these decisions as an adult, and those who tell me, "No one put a gun to my head," are right. But just because I acted as an adult doesn't mean I acted with wisdom, and the same is true of the men involved.

But a man who commits adultery lacks judgment: whoever does so destroys himself. Blows and disgrace are his lot, and his shame will never be wiped away.

Proverbs 6:32-33

Private-only relationships are not cute. And finally I had to look myself in the mirror and declare that I am better than this. No money could satisfy this void in my heart, nor could a quickie or a three-hour hideaway. The "weekend getaway sex rendezvous" was not worth the hours it would take. I felt empty and separated from myself. Low self-esteem, or not knowing how valuable you are, can alter your entire life.

If you are a Private Only girl, know that your path in life may be this today – but tomorrow, or the next minute, it can change. I know. I tried it. And it all begin with me telling myself that losing me is never worth it.

The Holding Pattern

I was on a plane traveling to Los Angeles when the

pilot made an announcement: "We have been told by Air Traffic Control that LAX is congested and there is no space at this time to land, so we have to be in a holding pattern for 15 minutes."

A first-time flyer asked the question, "What is a holding pattern"? The airline stewardess said, "Well, for lack of a better term, it's when the plane flies around in the air round and around. The only good thing is it will be only 15 minutes until we have clearance to land. There is no space for us right now at the gate."

Sound familiar? I thought, wow, this holding pattern sounds just like my life. How many of us find ourselves in holding patterns, flying around in a circle waiting for an opportunity to land safe and secure, to land our dreams, to land our hearts, to land our careers, to land our pain, to land our concerns, to land our insecurities, to land our weights, to land our thoughts? All of us at some point in our lives want to get out of the same scenery.

This is the relationship where you make a pact to wait! Wait for the children to get out of school. Wait until I talk to her, she's going through a lot right now. Wait until the right time. Wait until I get some things paid off, because I don't want this bill to be over my head. Wait until . . .

These are the most tantalizing relationships because there are some who wait and get who they have waited for, and then there are those who wait and never get what they wanted.

Which do you think is more likely when you go into a holding pattern with a man who's in covenant with someone else? You know the answer. He's keeping you in the secret zone and he's never going to be in position to really fulfill a commitment to you. My point here is not to beat up the man because he's not who I'm talking to. I'm talking to you, sisters. You cannot and should not accept this, but if you do, it's your responsibility. You did it to yourself.

And if you stay in this pattern long enough, you won't

even trust the men who do want to commit to you, who do want to care for you, who do want to make a covenant with you.

So you have to break that pattern and take back your life. Speak positive affirmations over your life and stop thinking of yourself as worth so little that you have to settle for the status of secret lover, or private-only relationship, or holding pattern. That is not who you were ever meant to be, and you should not agree to live that way one day longer.

Chapter Four

Meet the Players:
Provocative, Prolific and Passionate

"Watching you walk out of my life does not make me bitter or cynical about Love. But rather makes me realize that if I wanted so much to be with the wrong person how beautiful it will be when the right one comes along...." – Anonymous

There is no one description of the woman who gets involved with a married man. But there are profiles that many such women fit, and over the years I've seen quite a few of them more than once.

In this chapter, I want to introduce you to some of these profiles, and I'll start with one that I must tell you I identify with far too closely.

The Strong Woman

I saw all kinds of traits within myself I could no longer tolerate, and I identified many of the traits that made men gravitate to me. It was both revealing and terrifying.

Really being a strong woman is an attitude as much as anything else – a possession of your soul that sometimes leads to an "I got this" mentality, and other times causes you to well up with pride. If you're not careful, you can fail to see the distinction between being truly confident and simply being determined not to be broken.

I exhibit a lot of tenacity – setting goals and striving to accomplish them, raising my children alone, generally going through hell and back and living to tell you all about it. When you've gone through all that, it's not surprising that you would erect a power wall of protection around yourself – the kind that makes declaring in a subliminal conversation with yourself, "I will never put myself in the place to get played again."

We as women often handle things in our lives like that. I have met many women who rehearse this statement to me, and they come across to others as mean, aggressive, dominating and overly controlling.

But that's not the worst part. This is: Women like that become projects for many men. Their only objective is to break you, and once they succeed, they're done with you because you are no longer a challenge.

Then there are the men who are intimidated by the strong woman, making us constantly lament that we can never meet anyone who isn't.

But good men love women who portray confidence and intelligence. A confident, career-driven, stable and consistent man who is in touch with who he is will not mind sharing his life with a confident and positive woman. But he does not want to compete with a woman who does not know how to be a woman. If you get to the point where you and your will are so overpowering – where you may look and dress like a woman but your spirit overpowers like a man – it starts to feel to the man like he's just loving another man.

They're not going to find that appealing.

I have had men compliment me on my ability to be multi-faceted. My countenance made them think, "I want to see what she is about."

Of course, at the same time, I was endeavoring to let every man who crossed me know that I was on to their games. I was going to have my life my way, and he would be invited onto my dream team but he definitely could not coach the game. I exerted confidence in the ugliest way. If I received a compliment, I would respond with a highly sarcastic thank you.

The only way you were invited into my world was by your status. In retrospect, I was bitter, angry and broken with a vengeance. I could do badly all by myself, so why would I need a man?

One day I was at work when a particular gentleman came over to me and said, "Hello, how beautiful, are those your eyes?"

I replied very sternly: "Yes, they are."

He then said, "Whew, who hurt you?"

Immediately I went into game mode. That's all this is, after all. A game. So I flirted with the possibility of his interest, but because I always seemed to be number two, I could not see it as genuine interest. He would often come to the store to see me, and would ask me, "Ane, how is your day going?"

That was both interesting and weird to me. I wanted to be this strong woman determined to prove who I was, not realizing I had become a persona I'd created, and that was not a reflection of my true self.

Sisters, when we create super-woman mantles, we have to understand that capes come on and off. Super powers are artificial fillers to make us feel complete.

When you are in search for what you really are – your truest identity - you will learn how power really works in your life.

A woman who is really powerful, strong, beautiful, defined and intellectual understands her NEED in the world, and she can shift her strong nature into a powerful force to maximize and undergird the man who wants to make her a priority.

To make a long story short, I ran him off because I would always say things like, "Why do you want me?" or "I know you have other women", or "Who is calling you?"

I would suggest going to restaurants out of the way, until he asked me one day, "Ane, have you always been a man's secret?"

I said, "Isn't that what you guys do?"

"Who are you guys?" he asked.

"Men, period," I replied.

"No," he told me. "And until you think more of yourself than the man that's interested in you, your view of men will always be distasteful. You are a gorgeous woman, but your thinking is on another level, and I am sorry to throw water on your bitter princess party but I am too in control of my life to invite an angry woman who does not know who she truly is as a person."

I then began to think I could only attract the men who are attracted to my drama, or men who would tolerate me but keep me hidden because my insecurities would override my intelligence.

Men would be shocked that I would make certain statements:

1. All men are dogs, if they're not full grown there is a puppy somewhere in his nature.
2. I am so tired of men just wanting to sleep with me.
3. I want a man who loves me for me.
4. I want a man who wants to take care of me and protect me.
5. I want to be married one day, and if that's not your goal then I am not the one.
6. My life was good before you came and it will be good after you are gone.
7. I really don't need you. I have been taking care of me for years.

8. I am tired of every man I date always wanting me to be his secret.
9. I want to know what is in this for me.

And this drama list goes on and on. I was so strong that I forgot that I was a woman. Strong does not mean you are in control. The most healed place I could have ever tapped into for my life was to turn my strong nature into passion for purpose. With all this beauty on the outside, I was toxic on the inside. I knew how to dress and get an education, but I didn't know how to be a girl.

I did not know how to be dated or to be shown off, because I had settled for being a married man's strong woman. I was told that was attractive, so that's how I thought I had to be. My man needed me to be strong, I thought.

And he does, but not for the purpose of self-gratification. Too many women become the strong woman for a married man, or to a man who keeps you a secret but dates other women in the open. Sisters, you are allowing this because you don't know you're precious enough to be a showcase.

Find out what it is within you that is making you succumb to this unhealthy identity about your beautiful self. I got tired of hearing, "Baby, I need you to be strong for me, for us, for what we are creating."

I would say, "OK, I can do this." I would create another lie that would help me to hold on for another day. It became tedious and too much work and I knew it was a lie. I became deceived by my own thoughts. I ignored signs of inconsistent stories, and I ignored what my inner spirit was saying to me.

By now there comes a point in the relationship when it becomes extremely hard to walk away from him and it. You have fights you can't explain. You argue, threaten and give the man ultimatums.

When a man feels that kind of pressure, he escapes! He

sees his "strong" woman becoming unglued, not realizing he was attracted to what I created not what God created. I gave you the part of me I wanted you to know, not the part of me I desired for you to touch.

I can remember going to our church counselor and telling her I believed I was crazy. I felt like I was losing my touch with reality. I was out of control; I was becoming withdrawn. I lost my stride, I lost my desire to live, I became depressed, I didn't want to get out of bed –always crying and calling him, and asking when I was going to see him again.

I could feel him pulling away, and now I was wondering what I was going to do.

What was I doing? I didn't know myself anymore. I was calling in to my job, on the verge of being fired because my life had become all about him and me. After months of dating, we went a week without talking on the phone. I couldn't take it. I asked him, "I thought we were here for each other, why haven't I heard from you? So I guess you're falling back in love with your wife, so what am I going to do?"

He said, "BE STRONG, you will be fine. And Ane, I have a lot going on and I never expected you to be like this. What happened to us? Where is the woman that I met six months ago?"

After I politely let him have it with a particular choice of words, I slammed down the phone. I was crying and I said to myself, "I am telling his wife. That's what I will do."

So I called back and said, "I am going to call your wife."

"Call her," he said, "and if you do that, you would sound like every other stupid-a** woman that will be a woman scorned."

What in the world was going on with me that I had digressed into a woman who was spinning like a tornado with a vengeance? I found out in the days to come that I was not the only woman for him. There was another one, and another one and another one, and at the end of my journey into another shell of disgust and disappointment, I had to realize I still did not have him. And so what if he was falling in love again with his wife? That's his wife. I wasn't. My life with him was filled with hopes and could-be's and want-to-be's and what-if's and maybe-so's, and all the secret pillow-talk promises. And then one day your world can shift, which was the very thing I did not want to accept.

And yet there is nothing wrong with being strong. The issue is the motive and the intent of the message you are trying to portray. I have met and counseled women who are strong in nature, strong corporately, strong in their intelligence, strong in their passion for life, strong in God.

But they lack balance. A woman's strength has real power with the ability to be strong enough to be who she is, but to know how to tone it down in the right atmosphere. I remember when my husband and I were talking about a certain situation in our marriage, and I always responded, "Oh, I got it."

I would tell him, "Oh, I can't do this," when I felt like his reactions were not quick enough for me.

I was always suggesting better ways of doing things or a more "professional" smart way of achieving a solution, until he had to tell me, "Babe, I appreciate your knowledge and your know-how, but Ane, just tone it down and allow me to show you that I got it."

I knew then that because of my fear of being dropped I would escape and handle it. I am learning so much how to not diminish who I am, but to know when to be a girl, a lady and a woman. I had to learn that every woman needs a covering of protection, because in some ways we have adopted the mind frame of a man. It became our model to build our personal lives and our professional lives as a man would, when God in His wisdom never intended to give women the qualities of a man.

The particular kind of drive and creativity He gave us – the identity – are distinctive to us and are always supposed to be. Many of us allow our upbringing to change these things, but His design is and has always been best.

I enjoy women who are positive but humble, forceful but prissy, powerful but knowledgeable about how to navigate her life and her relationship with her man. I like that kind of woman. Many strong women eventually adopt the type of language their men use. There's nothing wrong with that, but they should not become the man. They should be his partner.

The relationship should be interchangeable, which is why you must understand that in a relationship with a married man, you can give a lot but you will only receive mere portions of him. He cannot give you all of himself, so why would you settle when God wants to make you a corporate woman and the only thing you settle for is being the mailroom girl?

A woman's strength is like a janitor. A janitor has the most important job in a corporation, and they have the keys to everything. People ignore his intelligence, and don't appreciate that he has knowledge of all the dynamics of the business. He has power but he has a low profile.

Today the janitor is called a domestic engineer. His title changed but his position and power didn't. He still has the same power – if he understands what to do with it.

Maybe, sisters, we also have new titles. Maybe we're more powerful than we ever realized. There is nothing wrong with that. But learn how to be powerful when it is needed, and how to keep a low profile and remain a woman. Let the power you have control growth. Control yourself and your range of position.

A man loves a woman who "has it together" and keeps it together. I am so grateful that I am finally learning how to live without the walls and defenses that made me strong, but let me be myself. I began to recognize that a woman who is determined to be successful and sexy has nothing to do with being an overpowered force for reckless behavior. Take authority over your sassiness, so you can be sassy and classy

– a wealth of knowledge. Shock yourself and your circle, and empower your channels of influence.

If you are a part of a relationship that is making you powerful but ignorant, GET OUT. Cut it off. You are supposed to be valued, and a man is supposed to bring you confirmation and validation. He is supposed to make you his queen, not his secret strategy. This may not be your life, but it was mine, and it might be the life of your girlfriend, mother, sister, auntie and best friend.

I was and am a strong woman, but now that strength is better defined! I create possibilities and provoke potential. I can mentor vision. I will push you into what you think are limits. I have favor on my life, I can speak Ebonics to investments. I can have dinner with anyone from fast-food-minded individuals to caviar people. I am just that type of woman. But just because my exposure has made me smart and well-rounded does not mean I should be arrogant and intimidating.

I was well aware as I went through these experiences that my physical beauty combined with some attractive personality traits. I knew I could be appealing; I would flirt with powerful men because that gave me greater access to knowledge. Or I did, until God revealed to me, "Ane, that's not what I require."

Sometimes I would push these secret men to improve themselves, and sometimes they would. But these men were not meant for me, so their wives or families or whoever else was benefiting from my influence. I got portions, if anything.

It aggravated me, but what else could happen when you're giving your best to people who can't even acknowledge their connection to you? You might get a private thank-you or perhaps a gift, but this sort of thing is suicide to your true destiny.

Sisters, I was pouring my fuel into the wrong cars. Don't do that. Pour your fuel into the right car and work your way back to healing yourself. That will allow you to focus on yourself, on your career, on your life, on your priorities – and you know what? The right man will come along to celebrate that openly, just as he will be able to genuinely celebrate who he is. And if any man can't or won't do that, you should ask why.

I once dated a single man for three-and-a-half years. I was the secret the entire time. His family didn't know about me, and while a few of his buddies did, I was NEVER invited into his world or to the parties he attended. I was invited to church functions because I was supportive and we were friends.

But that was it. The flag was waving in my face but I chose to paint it red, white and blue. Even if I would get angry, he knew the right words to say. I was this strong woman, but I was embarrassed of the way my circle was noticing my relationship. I had all the excuses at the ready: "It's just for right now!" "We'll come out when the time is right!"

Really.

Sweetheart, when is the right time? Please don't be a smart woman whose intuition is completely off.

But I LOVED HIM. At least that's what I told myself. We broke up and got back on with this silent commitment. We would not give our relationship a title but we knew we were together.

Foolery! You need absolutes, do you hear me, Sister? You need an absolute. You will always get what you set for yourself. Since you are so strong, be strong enough to redefine your relationship. Have limits. Draw boundaries, not walls.

Every woman lives to be the queen of her man's world. She wants to be his show piece and his trophy. A man loves it when his world knows that he has a good woman. It makes him stick his chest out and say, "Yes, I am the man." He loves accolades about his woman, and she does not need to be a secret sister.

Supposedly hindsight is always 20/20. So in hindsight

I see that when I was married, I maintained such a strong presence in the house that my husband probably didn't even feel like he was the man of the house. That doesn't excuse his cheating, but the self-evaluation is still important. It's part of what I contributed to the breakdown of the marriage, and if I want success in the future I can't pretend that didn't happen.

It had a lot to do with the fact that we stopped communicating effectively. I could hold conversations with everyone except him. And the more I felt I wasn't getting back what I deserved, the more I would shut him off. That strong, independent nature turned inward again, and I relied on what I was familiar with in order to function. Work was my strong suit, at least as I saw it, so I focused a lot on that. There was little use in trying to give him advice because he didn't receive it very well. Hindsight, of course, tells me that he probably felt I was treating him like a child and not like a man. That's how I was communicating it.

I was so much the tough girl that he couldn't even begin to try to satisfy me. He wanted me to walk in my own strength but not overpower him. I needed to trust that he had all of me but I didn't feel safe doing it. I can see how my success could have come across as prideful, although that was not my heart.

I had always thought that any man I would choose to connect to needed to accept who I was, success and all. Now I am learning how to still be me and not deflate. At the same time, I need to make sure I choose the right man whose heart I can trust with my success.

I have always been fearful of losing what I had worked so hard to establish. So I realized that my Strong Woman wall was stemming from a lack of trust. I also thought that loving was loving, and although I knew everyone had their own love language, my interpretation was all men love the same way, so I didn't love him with the understanding that all people are wired differently.

I wonder: Did I ever really take the time to find out

how to love him? Like many women, I am a multi-tasker, whereas he was a processor – and I often found his process wasn't fast enough for me. I measured his stride against mine, and his advances against mine. That wasn't fair. I was out in front of him when we should have been together.

For a man, it's difficult to feel excited about his home if he's not the head. And with me taking on all the tasks and solving all the problems, I was failing to operate in the helper role God designed for me. I was strong to the point of being rigid, and I couldn't adapt as he needed me to.

Our conversations invariably focused on what he wasn't doing, and why it wasn't enough in my eyes. This has really given me a new perception on appreciating the measure of a man. I told myself this: "Ane, you married him and you were not blind or dumb to the incompatibilities that were red flags in the relationship."

I loved and was in love with him, but as I finally figured out, I didn't know what to do when he asked for what he needed. Slowly but surely, we were disconnecting, and because I had faith in his word toward me and our vows, I felt certain our journey would not include adultery.

But we had a significant void and I was not easy to talk to. To me, everything was priority. I did everything but listen – and then there was an ear that was available.

"A MAN LOVES IT WHEN HE KNOWS HE HAS A STRONG WOMAN, AND SHE KNOWS HOW TO COVER HIS WEAKNESS AND PRESENT HIM AS BEING IN CONTROL OF EVERYTHING. EVERY MAN WANTS TO BE THE EMPIRE OF HIS FAMILY." EVERY MAN, IN SOME FACET OF HIS MANHOOD, RELIES ON HIS WOMAN'S STRENGTH.

The scripture says: "Her husband is so satisfied with her conduct towards himself, his household, his business, and their children, that he praiseth her. He shows himself sensible of her excellence, and encourages her, in her work, by the commendations he bestows."

TAKE YOUR LIFE BACK AND LIVE

Proverbs 28:31(Clark's commentary bible)

The Black Widow Spider

Here is what a company called Mountain Pest Control tells us about the Black Widow Spider:

The black widow spider has potent neurotoxin venom, and is considered the most venomous spider in North America. But the female injects such a small dose of venom that it rarely causes death. Reports indicate human mortality at well under than 1 percent from black widow spider bites.

Mating takes place in spring or summer. A common misconception is that the female usually consumes the male after mating. That rarely occurs. The black widow spider is a cobweb builder whose silk is very strong. The female constructs a web of crisscrossed silk threads with no recognizable pattern and with a dense area of silk, usually to one side, that serves as the spider daytime retreat. At night, the female hangs belly upward in the center of the web. She does not leave her hidden web voluntarily. The web typically is situated near the ground in a dark, sheltered site.

Bite Symptoms

The bite of a black widow spider initially may go unnoticed, but some people report a short stabbing pain. At first, there may be slight local swelling and two faint red spots, which are puncture points from the fangs. Pain soon begins and usually progresses from the bite site to finally localize in the abdomen and back. Severe cramping or rigidity may occur in the abdominal muscles. Other symptoms may include nausea, profuse perspiration, tremors, labored breathing, restlessness, increased blood pressure, and fever. Symptoms often diminish after a day or so and cease after several days. Serious long-term complications or death are very rare. A physician may administer a specific antivenin to counteract the venom or calcium gluconate to relieve pain.

I've known about this kind of spider for years. As I was

beginning my work on this book, I discovered that a lot of men refer to certain kinds of woman as a "she-devil." The more I read men's descriptions of what that kind of woman is like, the more I realized they were describing the Black Widow Spider to a T.

Since we looked at the description of what the actual spider is like, allow me to bring her out in a woman. The most intriguing fact about Ms. Widdy is her distinguished hour-glass shape. She is beautiful. But the male widow does not understand her ability yet. She is a spider who does not immediately kill her mate. Instead, she gives him time to produce, and when she feels that he is no longer able to supply for her, she kills him.

That's how many of my dear sisters are. They tunnel through life looking for their next victim – the one who can purchase them their Louis Vuitton, Coaches, Red Bottoms or Michael Kors. Or their next car payment. This poor sucker is going to be made responsible for what these women fail to build for themselves. They have no values, no heart of conviction and no sense of anyone but themselves. It's all about them.

They will chase men who have paper – or men who appear to have it – and they're big fans of men in power.

That's the Black Widow. She's seductive and intellectual. She mates with the male, who is bigger than she is, and swiftly takes control of the situation – which is amazing because she has a false sense of submission. She plays the game to get into the game. Her objective is to get what she can out of you and then leave you broken-hearted.

I have witnessed men in leadership positions who dated this kind of woman. The women were their secrets, until they eventually destroyed their legacy. We've seen it in government, in pulpits, in sports. It doesn't matter if it affects white-collar, blue-collar or no-collar homes. It affects them all. And the Black Widow doesn't care where she hides. She builds her nest out of sight and out of mind. Being the other woman is fine with her. She'll be quiet and protect your wife, your children and your career as long as you're supplying her with what she wants.

One thing that's unique about black widow spiders is that they are the only ones who build their nest close to the ground rather than up in the trees. That's so they can hide themselves. They strive on being inconspicuous. They also build their webs two-fold, with a great deal of silk. Why? Because that makes for a web that's very inviting – and very hard to get out of.

Sound familiar? These divas never leave their webs involuntarily. Instead, they invite their prey into their world of silk and satisfaction – only to lay with him and get pregnant – with his dreams, with his secrets, with his dissatisfactions about his wife, with his treasures.

Getting pregnant – both literally and metaphorically – is how she empowers herself to destroy him later. She has no intention of being a partner to him. The men, though, don't see that. They're so enthralled by her hour-glass shape they don't understand their time is running out.

By the way, I can understand if you're wondering right about now if I'm describing my own alter ego. I wondered myself at times if I ever let myself become the Black Widow. I examined myself hard.

But I realized, much to my relief, that I didn't because even in my darkest experiences I had conviction – which is not to say I did nothing wrong, but I didn't share Ms. Widdy's tactics or motivations.

In the church world, we call this woman a Jezebel. She doesn't kill her man immediately, but she breaks him down, uses his own strategy against him and ultimately destroys him. She doesn't threaten him until he starts losing his ability to provide for her. But when she starts, it's nasty. She'll go through his phone to get his wife's number. She'll make sure to sex him up when his wife is calling – just to put him in a vice. She'll show up somewhere public with no panties and send him a text to make sure he knows about it. Oh, and she'll repeat back to him what he told her his wife doesn't do during sex.

The man has made a commitment to protect his covenant. She is diluting his understanding of that commitment. And before that can be allowed to go too far, he needs to run, because she is never satisfied, and is motivated by nothing but self-gain. She is a ride-or-die girl. She'll ride with you while she can, or until she gets bored with you, but will go back into hiding and spin another web while you die.

Are you a Black Widow? Consider:

1. Do you become violent when the man cannot give you your way?
2. Do you sit and think of ways to manipulate him, crying and making up ways to make him come to your web?
3. Do you subliminally project questions about your relationship with him around his circle of influence, especially his wife?
4. Do you control him with sex?
5. Do you bring him into a world of perversion just so that he will create dissatisfaction for his spouse?
6. Do you scheme with him to plan out-of-town vacations so that you can brag about where you are traveling?
7. Do you lie about how much you love him, when you really just love what's in his pocket?
8. Do you enjoy seeing him weak so you can tell him that's where you want him to be?
9. Do you like having the map to his dynasty and holding it as a promissory note for manipulation?
10. Do you purposely make him miss important scheduled dates because you want him to be with you?

The strangest fact about the Black Widow's venom is that it enters your bloodstream, but it doesn't kill you. It just takes over your life.

The man who lets this woman in will see the impact on his ability to love and care for his family, to advance in his career, to function in his church and of course, to love his wife. He takes on a new persona because the venom has corrupted his nervous system.

And everyone loses in the process.

The Black Widow who becomes mistress to a powerful man loves the fact that he is complex, because she gets into the challenge. That's part of what drives such a conniving woman.

I've talked to many sisters who fit the description of Black Widows. Some of them wanted to change. Others rationalized that this is the way men have been treating women for years.

So they go about destroying his ability to dream, and to turn his dreams into reality. That's especially lethal because powerful men are always big dreamers. They dream and then they create what their dreams inspire. When a man loses his ability to create, he loses his passion, and soon he can no longer be productive.

In Genesis 1:28, God told Adam to multiply and be fruitful, to have dominion, to replenish. God provided him with specific instructions for success, well-being, growth and re-establishment. The secret word that was hidden is (replenish) – that word means to refill, restock and to reload. God gave every man the potential to come back, but it is a difficult path to re-chart when a man now has to take an unfamiliar approach. Trust is broken, relationships are broken, children get out of control, and the list goes on and on.

But why would he need to replenish in the first place when he was given everything he needed in the first place?

Even God sets up a plan for the future. In fact, no one does it better than God. He was giving man a system, a method for life. After the fall, when Adam and Eve had been expelled from the Garden of Eden, man was heartbroken and felt the need to protect his own. He had to till the ground with the memory of what he had lost still fresh in his mind. What he had once had power over had become off limits to him.

Sisters, I plead with you, don't mess up another woman's garden. Don't be the serpent! I know women will read this and wonder why I'm not directing my scrutiny at those no-good men. Because this book isn't for men! It's for women, and it's designed to help you gain control over the things that happen in your life. You may have no control over who approaches you, but you can control how you respond.

And for those who insist on clinging to the Black Widow persona, it's worth asking why they consistently fail to control their responses in a healthy way. I've asked many of them that very question, and here's what I've learned:

Its roots are in anger, and in the hatred of men in authority. These women love what these men represent, but they hate the men themselves. In many cases, it's because they remind them of their fathers, men who were providers but were never really there.

If this is you, you can be better. The first step to healing is confronting the truth about who you are – the hidden ills we don't want anyone to know about. Sometimes we can be the catalyst to our own self-destruction because we refuse to expose ourselves to ourselves.

One of the unhealthiest states is to be sick and dangerous and unaware of it. If you have seen yourself in this woman, I recommend you get help. Go to your pastor, your spiritual advisor, your mother, your sister – whoever is willing to tell you the truth and find the root in you that drives you to be this type of person.

You can live again. It may take time to peel back all your layers but your first step is to get out of the relationship before it is too late. You need to cut it off because he is probably afraid to cut it off with you. Be nice, be sensitive, and remember it is more than you that is tied to that man.

Trust me that there is someone who is assigned to you to help you heal your life again. You are still a beautiful woman, and you still have potential but you have to want to get better. Ask yourself, "Mirror on the wall, who's the problem in this all?"

The answer is you, so don't make every man pay for your past. When you heal your life, you will attract a different type of man.

And remember that you only want a man in authority because he brings a validation of your worth – and yet, he still keeps you a secret. What does that tell you?

Daddy's Girl

Have you ever talked like this?

"My dad was an awesome provider for our family. He validated me, he built me, he was there to commend me on everything. His presence was strong in our family. My dad gave our family a name. We can stand up with confidence in his name, and when I get married, my husband will have to understand that I am going to hyphenate my last name because I don't want to dishonor my father's worth."

This prima donna is a Daddy's Girl. Her identity is tied up in the father who provided for her and gave her affection, and that's exactly the kind of attention she wants from men in her life. She wants to see that sparkle in your eye and have it remind her of when she saw it in Daddy's eye. She wants glitz and glamour because this is the sort of thing that Princess was showered with as a little girl.

She sees him as a hero because he showed her how a father should love his little girl – and it's very nice that he did that, but often he neglected to show her some other things that were just as important. These include things that could cause her struggles in life, or situations in which she may not have everything she wants and she has to work out how to deal with it.

That would have only disappointed her, and that's the last thing Daddy would ever do to his little girl.

Like Barbie, Princess's house is a dream house in which there are always enough clothes, and they never get old. She never had to fight to get anything because it was always provided to her. And that standard Daddy set for how a man should treat her is the one she expects her man to live up to.

She may adapt to new realities but it won't happen easily. She's wired to think she shouldn't have to.

Look, we're all spoiled to some degree in our own ways. I am very much so. But my father did not create a life for me in which everything I wanted was simply given to me. For those whose fathers did, the men they meet face an extremely difficult challenge.

The man will have to compete with the father's dominance in her life. And that's even worse if the Daddy's Girl is your mistress and not your wife, because she will constantly demand your time. She expects you to make her your princess.

Some believe that if a father is in his daughter's life, "any kind of man can't turn her head." But that's not true. Some of the most astute ladies just hook up with the wrong kind of man, and these men are attracted to the Daddy's Girl aspects of their personalities. They can be told a lie and they will believe it because they learned through their daddies to trust men. They were taught that a good man would work hard for them, so they are willing to love him regardless of his other faults.

Princess is shocked when she finds out her wonderful boyfriend is married. She falls apart and can't function, going into a deep depression because she can't believe she could have been so stupid.

And yet it's hard for Princess to walk away because her father taught her loyalty. So the man will explain, you see, he really wanted to tell you, but the time was never right, and he's really unhappy in his marriage, and he really loves the time he spends with you, and he loves showering you with love.

He gets off on your excitement and energy, and the way you celebrate him in witty and fun ways. You thrive on his smile, and you acknowledge his successes. She affirms his approach to business, and the way he's such a get-it-done kind of guy.

And he recognizes in all this that you have a sense of dependency on him.

So as sensitive as you may be to his struggles, as much as you want to be the wind beneath his wings, as much as you want to be the consoler to the broken side of him – you are not his wife. God still honors the marriage covenant, and you are not included in it. You need to pull your heart back. And if you're not willing to do that solely on the basis of this simple truth, you should notice the signs. Your friends are probably pointing them out to you.

He texts you a lot more than he calls, and many days he tells you that because of his schedule a text is the best you can expect. You buy it because you saw the same behavior in your father.

And even when he's with you – even when he's making love to you, which he makes clear is heavenly – you'll see his priority as soon as his wife calls.

Is this you? Take your life back. There is someone out there who will value you for how you were raised, but will be man enough to introduce you to life as it really is, and will be a man of such character that you'll be happy to drop your daddy's name and take his.

Don't rob your inheritance. He is not going to raise you all over again. He is going to be your husband.

The Cheating Married Woman

One thing the cheating married woman is usually not after – at least as her primary motivation – is sex. That may be part of the affair, but that's not what she's really after. She's after something she wants, but isn't getting, from her husband. Maybe it's affirmation that she's beautiful. Maybe it's attention. Maybe it's some other form of fulfillment.

But the cheating woman follows very different patterns than the cheating man. She probably doesn't have her lover's number in her phone – not even disguised with codes or some sort of fake name. And she's very good at convincing her husband that her lover is really just a co-worker or even her brother.

Her behavior when she gets caught is interesting as well. She'll still cook and clean, wash her husband's clothes, rub his back and make love to him. She might even take her sexiness to another level with him – all while swearing to him through tears and promises in God's name that he is her only true love.

Meanwhile, she still has an awful lot of "meetings" and "special dinners," through which she's getting right back on track with her lover.

This is not because the cheating woman is overly sexual. It's because she is so emotional. Where the man is driven by productivity, the cheating woman is driven by emotion. And she notices things that trouble her emotionally. She notices that sex has become transactional. She notices that she and her husband get turned on by different things. She notices that he might demonstrate more passion for his career, his ministry, his sports teams, his video games . . . than he does for her.

And she hurts. She wants to find a way to get the fulfillment it's killing her not to get from him. So along comes another man who provides that very thing, and who accepts her – flaws and all. Maybe her marriage is abusive and he represents her escape from it. Maybe he makes her feel beautiful in a way her husband hasn't done in years.

If this is you, find a sister who can pray with you – and can advise you on ways to exit this building. You don't want to be there.

Remember, men are territorial, and as a result they cannot handle it when they find out their woman has cheated. That's why you see such rage in these situations – up to and including the murder of the cheating wife and sometimes even the children.

When I was married, my husband once told me,

"That's a major violation. Men cannot handle disrespect."

Proverbs 6:34 says the same thing: "For jealousy arouses a husband's fury, and he will show no mercy when he takes revenge."

But if men can't handle disrespect, women get tripped up when they look for men to provide them with what they should be able to find within themselves.

I was constantly declaring, "I just want to be happy" and putting it on my man that I wasn't, as if making me happy was his job. Not that he can't help, not that he can't add to my happiness by affirming me – of course he can do that and it's wonderful if he does – but no man can make me happy because I have to decide to be happy. I had to already know I was beautiful before he told me. I had to embrace my own self-esteem before he built me up.

Because if I couldn't do that, his compliments wouldn't resonate with me anyway. I wouldn't even believe them. They couldn't satisfy the drought in my heart. It never can for the cheating woman.

As for the men in the cheating woman's life, they usually fall into one of four categories:
1. Friend
2. Just a Friend.
3. Friend Friend.
4. Friend with Benefits.

Each of the four has his own recognizable characteristics, which I'll touch on here:

Friend

This is a man a woman will talk to when she is bored. She won't share intimate thoughts with him because she doesn't care if he is there or not. She answers him when she wants to, goes to dinner with him when she wants to and lets him serve as her time-killer. There a perfect understanding that "WE ARE JUST FRIENDS" although she knows he is into her and he might even raise the possibility every so often. But at the end of the conversation she always makes it clear there is no chance. He's just there to be used when she is upset with her husband – whom he probably knows and is cool with. Because hey, you're just friends!

Just a Friend

This man is mystical. She enjoys him a lot. He's cool. He rocks her conversations and laughs at jokes her husband thinks are ridiculous. He pays a lot of attention to her and she is willing to talk to him about her discontentment with her husband. He's got her sold on the idea that no one really understands her like he does.

He knows he can't have her but he will settle for the time she is willing to share. He probably even has a girlfriend – he can't have her, after all – but there's some jealousy in play and she might even find herself arguing with him, telling him he shouldn't be sleeping with his girlfriend or something silly like that. She's married so it's absurd that she's bothered by it, but she is.

People definitely notice the chemistry she has with him. They've "got each other's backs." They buy gifts for each other and lend each other money. And often they keep it a secret.

He will ask her what she did the previous night, and he's convinced that if she had been with him, he could have loved her better than her husband.

So does she actually sleep with him? Not often, but she does. She and Just a Friend know that "this is not right," but they flirt heavily and they text affectionate messages to each other. He'll even text her from church or other functions, telling her she's beautiful. He knows he's working within limitations so he gets as much as he can – and by the way, her husband is suspicious of him.

Friend Friend

This guy really makes her struggle. She debates whether she should walk away from the relationship or stay. She can't get him off her mind, and often he keeps her in the therapist's office.

This is the guy who is always coming to the altar for prayer. She looks at him and thinks he could have been her ideal mate if only she had waited for him – but it's too late for that now. Maybe she had a previous connection to him but they never quite closed the deal and now she's married to someone else.

Friend Friend pressures her. He challenges her about the condition of her life. He challenges her husband's ability to take care of her. He magnifies all the shortcomings of her spouse and she listens – all of which empowers her anger and dissatisfaction.

Sometimes Friend Friend will even create a secret bank account for her, so she won't have to struggle, and of course she'll know it's because of him. He will even take care of her children. He'll fawn over her and notice every little thing about her.

And he will get her in trouble. He might take a chance by texting her at night to see if she'll respond. He'll throw her off her rhythm. And however imperfect her husband may be, it is NOT worth it. Whatever you want to be different in your marriage, talk to your husband about it and work it out with him. Friend Friend cannot give you any of this, and he is not in covenant with you. However much his attention may excite you, it can never really fulfill you because only what you experience within the covenant God blesses can do that.

Friend with Benefits

You know what this is, and I don't want to spend a lot

of time on it because it doesn't deserve a lot. We're talking about two individuals who come together for no-strings-attached sex. This guy causes her to lose herself and her standard. He has no regard for her commitment to God or to her family, and she rationalizes it by saying she can't help the way he makes her feel.

This is a mess, but women do it. Maybe she has a freaky side but she doesn't want to let her husband see it, so she looks for a way to live out that fantasy with someone else. Benefits have to be renewed year after year, so the longer this lasts, the more she lies to family – all to protect nothing more than physical lust and sexual perversion.

Sisters, shut this down. Take the cookies back to your husband, full time. If there's a part of you he hasn't seen, introduce him to it and let him enjoy it. If there's something you want that pleases you, ask him for it and let him do it. He might surprise you. You might even find that he's been praying you'd give him a lap dance. God gave you the ability to be creative, so why give it to another man – which will guarantee God will not be pleased with how you use what He gave you.

Knock this off and work out your marriage, like they say, for real for real!

The Perfect Woman

Who wouldn't want the perfect woman? She has so many positive attributes. She's a business professional, an excellent money manager, highly composed and accomplished with a college degree. She can even handle basic car maintenance!

She sets markers for the progress in her life and she meets them. Who wouldn't want to be with her?

But that only works if she's really the right one, and if what you see is really an accurate picture of who she is.

The Perfect Woman usually got this way, at least in part, in response to some sort of rejection. It steeled her, made her militant. She became determined to show that she could take command of her life and achieve things, and she has — but there is never really a point where she feels satisfied by what she's done. Every achievement sets the marker back as she strives for the next goal. It's exhilarating, but her heart is very hard.

So why would a woman who has it all together like this get involved with a married man? You'd think her logical side would recognize the danger. I once had a Perfect Woman friend who did this very thing, and what she told me was that the affair offered her an outlet from the intense seriousness of her life — without the need for a serious commitment. They had an "arrangement" by which she would pencil him in for a hookup if her schedule permitted it. It might not be today. It might be Friday in Paris. But as long as they both understood the hookups needed to be fit in between other priorities, then their arrangement held.

But for the man who decides to have an affair with the Perfect Woman, he had better understand: She has no patience for nonsense. The man who likes to be frivolous or silly will find that his perfect mistress finds this side of him hard to take, because what she's come to respect is order, structure and strategy. If the man she's involved with doesn't show that, she might start acting more like his mother than his lover.

And that's the ironic thing about her using a married man as an escape from her seriousness. She can't really do it, because she needs to control everything and everyone around her. Even her relaxation has to fit into her structure and operate according to her larger plan.

This is not to say she won't make him feel good. She may very well make his world feel like the ambiance of Heaven at times. But she is so driven, she finds it totally acceptable to be in second place — and that's what messing around with a married man is. You're always in second place. So when she gets her heart broken — and that's inevitable when you're involved with a married man — she's going to turn around and make life that much harder for the next five men she gets involved with.

The Stripper

This woman is amazing! She's the one they talk about in barber shops and at private parties for men. Those statements that begin with, "I wish my wife would . . ." are about the things this woman is willing to do.

I once asked a male friend who was caught in a scandal with a woman like this, why he would have risked so much to hook up with someone who had nothing at stake but her pole. His answer surprised me: "Sis, I wanted to experience this with my wife but I knew she would reject me. I knew she was not open enough for me to give my fantasy to her. All I asked was for her to dress up every now and then, rub my head, tell me I am the man. I mean I work hard. Our life is nice. I am a good father. I am a great provider. I pay all the bills and all I ask of her is to come and let's try something new, be more inviting when a brother comes home. Talk sexy to me. Take some 'sexy classes' or something."

Even more surprising: His wife didn't leave him because she actually felt some of this was her fault for not listening when he expressed his desires. She figured it wasn't broken so there was no point in fixing it, and that helped set the stage for his cheating.

This got me thinking about what the job of a stripper really is.

Her "profession" brings men into an exotic mystery of passion. Her goal is to become that man's greatest desire for those few minutes of ecstasy. She provides a sense of comfort for his expression of his naughty nature.

It's an emotional high she'll deliver by tantalizing him and sleeping with him, and then she'll make sure she gets paid for it.

In Proverbs 31, the king's mother warns him about

women like this. Her heart is not with him, but rather she wants to get into his mind and have him desire the motion of her body. She wants to sell the man on her perversion so much that he craves it.

Her entire proposition is artificial. It's all about the man getting a thrill and paying handsomely for it – and yes, many do. And the men who have affairs with strippers soon start holding their wives to the same standard of erotic wildness that they're experiencing with their stripper mistresses.

But the stripper doesn't care about the man. It's all about the experience for her. It's about the moment. She'll do what he wants – wear his favorite color underwear, dress in his favorite outfit. It's his world and she just dances in it, so it's all about the performance for her.

For the man, meanwhile, it's often more mental and emotional than it is physical. He wants to feel that his woman will give him what he wants because he matters that much, and if he feels his wife will not, then he becomes easy prey for someone who will.

I became so interested in this phenomenon that I actually took a stripper class, much as that may shock some of you. I took pole dancing and lap dancing classes. They take you into a dark room, and it's like a trance. I felt conflicted about it and I asked the instructor, "Am I bad for acting like this?"

The instructor responded, "No ma'am, you are creating art for your husband."

I decided I would put that idea into action, and you don't need any more details about that.

But I was honestly nervous about whether he would like it or not. I had no need to be. He smiled and said, "If this is what men get in those clubs I can see why it is addictive."

It opened up another level of communication concerning intimacy and euphoria in our marriage, and it helped to make him more comfortable in sharing his thoughts without fearing that I would feel disrespected or objectified if he did.

I happily became his opportunity to express and experience every desire of his heart. There was nothing perverted or twisted about it. It was offered and enjoyed within a marriage blessed by God and it was wonderful. But that doesn't mean I became the stripper, because my heart was for him – not to control him or get him addicted, but to bless him.

And sisters, if you're not doing that for your husbands, you should really ask yourselves why.

I know what happens when you've been married for a while. You lose a bit of your desire to bring it. And you start fixating on things that never bothered you before. You don't like your weight. You don't like the way you look in lingerie. The children are keeping you too busy. You'll have sex but you might not put too much time and effort into making it special and memorable for him, because . . . well, you can come up with plenty of reasons if you really want to.

But you make time for lots of other things that you see as priorities. This isn't? Even if it would bless your husband and bring joy to his life? Even if it would fortify your marriage against the threat that stripper might pose? It's still not important enough?

It needs to be. Take the initiative. Talk to him and find out his thoughts on where things stand with intimacy in your marriage. What has he been dreaming about? What does he wish you would do, but is afraid to ask for? Let him know it's OK.

And set the stage. Leave sexy notes. Pick up an exotic drink you can share. Turn off the lights and light some candles. Play his favorite music. Maybe you want to record your own voice telling him just what he loves to hear, and let it play throughout the house.

By the way, you might find he doesn't even care that much about whatever is bothering you. Maybe he doesn't care if you've put on a few pounds, or if your bra and panties don't match. He just wants you to be his woman. So be! Kiss all over him. Invite him to touch you in that area where he's not sure he should. Undress him. Model for him. Tease him. Talk softly into his ear, and ask what he would like you to do.

And then . . . do it!

I know this may feel uncomfortable at first, but stick with it and you will find before long that you both will love it. It's better than the stripper. It's erotic love as God intended it, and as he put you together to enjoy with each other.

By the way, there might be times when he just wants you to go for a walk with him and listen to him. Do that too. You know why? Because the stripper listens too. She knows all the ways to work her way into his heart, so your job is to guard it each and every day. It's not for her, it's for you. So in every way possible, treat it that way. You'll never be sorry you did.

The Soloist

This is the sister who largely travels alone. She might have one or two friends but that's it. She is very secretive but she enjoys exploring and challenging emotions. Men like her because they figure her solo act limits their risk of exposure. She is most likely single with no children. She has her own place, her own car and her own career.

She is guarded, which makes her a bit mysterious to those who would like to figure her out. But she doesn't mind playing dual roles – the one you need her to play in public and the one where she can just relax and be herself. She is probably comfortable around conservative banker types – who tend to find her attractive – and she can hold her own in the "pearls and pumps" scene. She might relax to jazz music and champagne.

The Soloist will not give the man grief about being a

"good man," because she prefers that he maintain his patterns. If he needs to be with his wife and family – even for an extended family vacation – that's fine with her as long as she gets the occasional text to assure her that everything is good.

If there's one person she confides in about the relationship, it's probably her mother or a sister because that is the one safe haven she feels comfortable with. Otherwise she fiercely protects herself and her situation – and is careful to look after her own life so as to keep her man's patterns intact.

I've talked to women who fit this pattern, and I asked them how they could do what they were doing. One responded like this: "Ane, I know I am wrong and I should not be doing this, but there is no life or commitment and I like that. No pressure to perform! I still maintain my life and I am free to walk or stay. Do I love him? No, but do I love his company and I like him".

I asked, "What's the difference?"

She replied, "I know this is not going anywhere. This man loves his wife and I know that, so I have what I have of him and leave myself open to options."

Men are attracted to the fact that discussing his married life is totally off-limits with the Soloist. She refuses to rescue him from whatever problems he is having, but she will still enjoy him.

What she fears, however, is people knowing that she is in jeopardy of tainting her good name, which is one reason she is so unwilling to share her secret outside a very tight circle.

The Fool

This woman may be a man's greatest lover, but she is off the chain and it's a mystery why he wants to be with her. She'll beat his behind. She'll expect him to come by her house every pay day. She'll have a meltdown if he breaks a promise to her. She'll call him while he's out with his family and she doesn't care in the slightest.

And sometimes her behavior can get scary.

She has no real boundaries and she doesn't give him any room to maneuver. She wants to know exactly how many times he's made love to his wife this week. She demands to know why he took so long in the shower. She will text or even call him at all hours of the night. And if he doesn't give her exactly what she wants, there is no telling what she might do. I've seen these women set men's cars on fire. I've seen them send the man's wife a birthday card and sign it, "Your husband's mistress."

Oh yes. They do that. And I'll be honest here. I once fell into this role myself. The man I was seeing wasn't even married, but I was so convinced he was stepping out on me with someone else that I would go through his phone and even follow him. I ripped up all his sweaters once when I didn't like what I found.

Thank God for grace and maturity!

I don't care how beautiful this woman is. Men are playing with fire when they get involved with the Fool. She will not only threaten at every turn to expose him, she will threaten his wife, his children. She wants attention from him and can't get enough of it – and because he has a wife and a family, he can never give her as much as she wants.

He might as well be lighting the fuse to a bomb.

So why do men get involved with women like this? Well, they don't walk around wearing nametags that say, "Hi, I'm a fool." She is probably very beautiful, and she might very well be an accomplished professional woman. She does not necessarily give outward signs of being insane – at least not right away.

But the man who gets involved with this woman will soon find out: She is an angry woman full of wrath and rage, and it won't be long before he feels it.

The Baby Mama

Obviously this woman has children, and the men who date her understand that they will eventually become the secret daddy. This is certainly not every single mother – I was one myself, after all – but it's hardly surprising that many women are motivated to find a father for their children, or at least someone who is willing to play the role when he can.

Taking on this woman as a mistress may seem virtuous because a man may do things for the children, even support them financially. But ultimately it's a disservice to everyone who's involved in the situation – the children included.

On the most basic level, the mother needs to understand that the children do follow her lead. She is modeling for them. And while she might try to hide her involvement with a married man from them – seeing him only when they're asleep, etc. – children are not stupid. They notice when they're mother seems to be hiding something, or not telling them the whole story about what's going on with her.

Think about the example this sets for a daughter. It's one thing if you've had children out of wedlock, or if you're now divorced. That's done and there's no changing it. But if your plan to provide for your children is to sleep with a married man, what does that say to your daughter about what your priorities are – and about what hers should be?

As for her sons, why would she think they're going to learn the value of faithfulness in marriage when her own behavior says she doesn't respect another person's marriage?

If a single mother can't find a job, she is better off getting on the welfare system than she is sleeping with a married man. For one thing, that money may be nice, but what makes her think she can count on it over the long term? He is not her husband! He has not made a long-term commitment to her and he is never going to do so. That money that's paying the bills or buying the clothes and the groceries is going to be sorely missed when he decides it's just too complicated or no longer worth it to bankroll her.

Even worse, she needs to think about how it affects the children when the affair gets exposed – and she'd be a fool to assume it won't. Secrets come to light. It's how life is. And when she is revealed as a party to adultery, that stigma will also fall on the children whether it's fair or not – which it obviously isn't. Doesn't matter.

It's also not fair to tell the children things like, "What happens in our house stays in our house." They're not responsible for her indiscretion, and they don't deserve the burden of having to hide it for her. She's putting them in a position where they may feel they have to lie to protect her, and that is not only contrary to what she should be teaching them, it's a responsibility they are in no way ready to take on.

The single mother is better off baking cookies and selling them than she would be sleeping with a married man.

I know, because I put my own children through this. It was selfish of me to burden my children with my secrets, and I deeply regret doing it.

And no single mother should think this is the only way to provide for her children. Develop a strategy. Work it. Stay committed to it. Don't give up when it gets hard and you experience rejection. Your children deserve your best, and sleeping with a married man is not your best!

Finally, understand this: If the children meet this man (especially if they do not have a close relationship with their biological father) he may represent for them the potential for that void to be filled. They see in him the possibility of completion. That is cruel to your children because his commitment is elsewhere. And the man who would leave his biological children to raise the children of a mistress (yes, I've seen it happen) is not the kind of man you want!

Girl, shake yourself! I ultimately apologized to my children for what I put them through. The brokenness they saw in me did not paint a good picture for them.

The man you – and they – deserve is one who understands commitment and can give it to all of you fully.

The Artist

Here we have a sister who is creative in her methods of making her man enjoy life. Sensitive and gentle in character, men enjoy giving her their love. She is not argumentative but she knows how to express her frustration, and can reach a compromise with a man because she aims to please. That's no small thing. Show me a woman who can easily compromise without an attitude and I'll show you a flying pig.

The man who chooses The Artist as his mistress will probably fall in love with her because she probes him with questions designed to help her understand how to give him what he wants. He will enjoy her interest in him, which she uses to introduce him to new ideas and new ways to make him smile.

And she'll act like she's on a mission about it too. She'll take him back to his childhood and ask questions like:

1. Babe, tell me two things as a boy you desired and you never received? Then she goes out and purchases the items and has them as a surprise when she sees him. She makes him blush.
2. What can I do to make your day flow better? Then she will make sure she provides that for him that day, even if it's having lunch at a certain time because his schedule is too hectic.
3. Tell me something as a teenager you did and you never told anyone. She'll laugh at his secret. She makes him feel relaxed and not judged. She knows how to be his friend.

He loves this. The Artist will make him reminisce about his life while she laughs with him and feels what he feels. And while her interest in him is genuine, she will be in an internal battle over it. She knows the relationship is wrong and she should walk away from it, but she is in tune with him and she does not want to let him go.

She would be ideal as the secretary/administrator for a pastor, or the right-hand woman to a governor. She looks at the man in her life with adoration, and sees everything she's making with him as art. Every man wants to feel like he is adored and she is an expert at making him feel that way.

But here's the problem: She is not loving who he really is, because that's the guy who's home with his wife. It's easy for her to act like the girl who makes him say, "Where has she been all my life?" This is true even though she may not have sex with him for months. What develops instead is a very deep, emotional soul tie. She'll pay attention to everything from the missing button on his shirt to his favorite song. She's creating art, and it's an expensive commodity by the time he's finished with it.

Finally departing from this sister will leave him an emotional wreck. They created a painting together and only they know what went into that painting. She pulled out of him things that his wife may have missed or ignored for years. She made him feel alive and vibrant. He'll even go to dinner with her and never mention that his wife already cooked, because he wants to be a part of what they've created. She'll turn down gifts from him, insisting that they are not what the relationship is about.

This relationship is so intense that he will really think about walking away from everything he's built for her. Something in him has been tapped, and he won't want to lose that moment. She'll even assure him that as he goes through the difficult journey of leaving his spouse, she'll be with him every step of the way.

The men who get involved with the Artist are typically the "good" men that no one would ever expect to do such a thing. What she offers is that appealing.

But here is where it all breaks down: Although she may

fit in his life, she will never really be accepted into his world. Even if he were to leave his wife for him, she would never really feel comfortable at family gatherings or in his social circle. She would be miserable – and suddenly that beautiful painting they built together won't be enough to bring either of them the happiness they were looking for.

And it's always easier to be the Artist when someone else is really responsible for the commitment.

The Woman Scorned

Not every woman can handle a breakup, and this woman will present a man with a part of her that he will not be able to control. She becomes vengeful. She feels she invested time in him that has now proven to be wasted, and having been dumped, she now feels disrespected and taken advantage of.

But it's worse than that. She's after, in the legendary words of James Brown, The Big Payback. She'll do things that even she probably never thought she would do. The pain she feels is inexplicable and she wants to make sure the man who scorned her feels every bit of it.

I remember talking to one woman who had just found out her boyfriend was married, and she told me flat out that she was seriously considering showing up at his workplace and shooting him.

"For what?" I asked. "What would that solve?"

With tears rolling down her face, she yelled, "HE HURT ME! HE LIED TO ME!"

I tried to stay rational in my response: "Yes, I understand, but there were signs. We all knew something was up. Even you knew it, but you chose to ignore it."

The fact that she should have seen the signs is hardly going to make things better at this point, but she should have seen them. Sisters, please do not allow yourselves to walk into the deceit of a relationship that flows like this:

1. He says he will text you at a specific time
2. He says he will turn his phone off at night
3. "Don't call me, I will call you."
4. Let's go to dinner, he says, and he takes you about 10-15 miles outside the city
5. Your number is not even programmed in his phone, and if it is, it's under a male's name
6. His time is restricted with you
7. You cannot come to his job
8. He steps outside to answer his phone when he is with you and he says it's a business call
9. He goes into the bathroom to talk
10. He sends you roses but does not sign his name
11. He asks you to get a room in your name and assures you he will take care of it
12. He takes you on a business trip with him but flies you separately
13. He flies you into his city to see him, and the only time you see him is in the day and for dinner at night
14. He spends a weekend with you but tells you not to tell anyone where you are going together
15. He asks you to keep your relationship private because he does not want anybody in his business

Why these rules, especially with no explanation? Because you are his secret. Do you want to be the secret? Sisters, you must remember that you are fragile beings – made from a rib. You are easily broken and you cannot afford to keep being broken by the same kind of men. Many of you will find yourselves asking, "Why do I find myself in this same situation again?"

I'll tell you why. Because you have not healed the area that keeps attracting the same type of man. And when you move on to a different man, you will find that he has the same type of spirit.

You may feel like killing him, but you must know that will be of no benefit to you. You're going to make him the victim and turn yourself into the perpetrator. That might feel powerful in the moment, but what is it going to do to your life?

And even if you settle for stalking him and tormenting him, you still make him the victim because now he's protecting his family from you.

Often the woman scorned will contact everyone to tell them about the affair, so the man who chose this type of woman as his mistress had better be prepared to fess up to his wife on his own terms. But it won't stop there. She'll send a letter to his church, to his boss, to other family members. She will find a way to make her wrath felt.

She will call his phone and leave obscene messages, and inform him in no uncertain terms, "I hate you!"

I've counseled women who had just been told by the man that he simply couldn't do the relationship anymore. I've had to persuade them not to destroy him. Some finally accept it and just go through the pain quietly, and it's all the more difficult because the relationship was a big secret in the first place, so there are not that many people in whom she can confide.

By the way, the men sometimes make it worse. They'll say they have to end it, but then they'll feel guilty and call to see how she's doing. That does not help. Men, if you end it (which you should, of course, because your commitment is to your wife), then let it be done. You're not making her feel better if you tell her you miss her. It's hard enough to accept the end of it without getting signals like that from you.

The worst scorned-woman scenario is the one in which a child was conceived from the relationship. As her hatred of the man rises, the child is trapped in derision and misery. Both of them regret what happened and the child becomes the object of that regret.

That is not fair.

What the scorned woman needs to do is accept what is necessary and release him back to his life, because that's where he belonged in the first place. Take yourself back, love yourself and live. Forgive yourself. And stop accepting portions, which is all a married man can ever give you.

One of my favorite Scriptures is Psalm 139:14 (AMP): I will confess and praise you for You are fearful and wonderful and for the awful wonder of my birth! Wonderful are Your works, and that my inner self knows right well.

I use this version because it's your inner self that has to know your value. Even if you're hurting because the relationship ended, you need to know that your inner self is stronger than you can possibly imagine. If you are in an unhealthy relationship now, your inner self will empower you to pull it together and fortify you as a woman. Set boundaries, call the shots in your life, and make a decision to do better because your value demands it.

I don't know the author of this quote, but I want you to remember it: "We can only be said to be alive in those moments when our hearts are conscious of our treasures."

The Social Media Lover

The profile of a person you meet on social media may have little to do with the way that person really is. People design their social media profiles to sell themselves to you, to show you a version of themselves that you would hopefully find appealing.

You would think people would know this, and that it would suggest caution when getting into social media romances. But it's amazing how often people fall into this strange trap – and how often they actually lose their marriages because of something that started on social media.

Let's say this upfront: There's a lot good that happens because of social media. I think it's great that old classmates can reconnect so easily. I've seen old friendships rekindled in a healthy and joyous way, and I've seen entire classes reestablish their bonds in a way they never could have without the role social media played.

It's also a lot easier to follow the updates of your cousins, aunts and uncles on Facebook than it is to call them all the time to find out the most trivial details of their lives. Not that the calls don't have their place, but let's be honest, this is a simpler and often less-intrusive way of keeping up to speed on the people we care about. That's all to the good.

Like any other tool, social media is only as good or bad as the way people use it. But even within the context of the generally positive things described above, there is danger.

Who is a bigger temptation than the person you dated (or wanted to date but never quite worked up the nerve to ask) 20 years ago? What if they look even better today? What if they were cold to you in school but they're surprisingly friendly now? What if you're finding that you're clicking with this person in a way that's fresher and more exciting than the way you're clicking with your spouse?

Maybe Facebook is the way you put the bad high school breakup behind you and make peace. Maybe it's the venue through which you confess the secret crush you didn't dare admit back in the day? (And maybe you discover to your surprised delight that the crush was mutual.)

You can see where this has the potential to go, and it doesn't necessarily have to involve people from your past. People get chatty over social media all the time for various reasons.

Married men do not fail to notice the attractive photo of a woman, and no matter how committed they may feel they are to their wives, they will engage in conversation with that woman just about every time if prompted. They probably don't intend to do anything wrong – at least not at first. But they're treading on dangerous ground.

It is very easy for that woman to make the man feel alive and excited through the safety of her computer. She doesn't have to fix his meal, take care of the kids, deal with how late he works, listen to him snore . . . all she has to do is talk to him and show interest.

And women are smart. They can look through your

photos and see how many pictures a man has posted of himself with his wife. They can see how often he talks about her. You can learn a lot about a person's marriage from what's emphasized – and not emphasized – on social media.

If a woman is looking to entice a man via social media, she can learn about his likes and dislikes, about his interests and frustrations. And probably a lot about his life and his family.

Women can do something else, too. They can make themselves look good, sometimes better than they do in real life. This isn't that difficult. She crops the headshot just so. Or she uses a photo that's 10 years old. Or a photo that's not even her. She lists personal information that makes her sound enticing and fun.

Men fall into this trap a lot. They'll get to the point where the primary reason they're getting on their computer is to see if that woman is there to pay attention to him. And remember, most affairs don't start with sex. They start with attention, or affirmation, or empathy. They start because the woman is providing something for the man that he feels he's not getting in his marriage, and he keeps coming back for that. This is disturbingly easy over social media because they don't have to arrange get-togethers or even talk on the phone. Some of it might even be out in the open: He posts, she comments. She posts, he likes. Maybe his wife is friends with her too. What she can see doesn't necessarily appear to be cause for alarm. But what she doesn't see is the real problem.

And these days it's so easy to delve into social media on your smartphone, a man doesn't even have to open up his laptop or sit down at his desktop computer to interact with this woman.

There is actually a website called Facebookcheating.com that claims Facebook is responsible for one out of every three divorces. A Boston University study suggests that people who use Facebook are 32 percent more likely to leave their spouses.

As with all studies, it's hard to tell if the correlation proves a cause, but common sense would suggest that social media is at least a potential minefield for anyone who is married.

One good safeguard is for married couples to openly share their Facebook and smartphone passwords with each other. I'm sure that most couples in strong marriages would be reluctant to actually look – surely feeling that their actions are suspicious and maybe even a bit paranoid – but seriously, would you be as likely to engage in that chat session if you knew your spouse had your password and could check?

Maybe it's the reason you never start down that road in the first place.

And sisters, if you're the Social Media Lover – the woman who enjoys the sport of enticing men via the Internet – do yourself and everyone else a favor and check his wife's profile too. You might find photos of them together, or of their children. At the very least, get to know something about the woman you'll be hurting if you decide to play this game. Then back away, and don't. Use social media to strengthen family ties and good friendships, and let the man's marriage be.

One Final Word About the Other Woman

I know you hate the other woman. You want her dead and out of the picture. I did too. But I have lived on both ends of this broom, and neither is easy.

That's why I'm going to briefly defend the other woman. She may well have been trifling to be in this triangle with your husband, but you never know what lies she was made to believe about you. Her idea is to give him what (at least she thinks) he is not getting at home. If he feels deflated at home, he will go where he feels superior. She wants to give him what he wants but can't get from you.

I have asked many women why they fooled around

with married men. Two answers are most common. First, they say they didn't know he was married. Second, they say that messing around with a married man is a way to avoid commitment.

Ladies, you need to understand the dynamic at work here. He is open and vulnerable, and so is she. No matter what people say, opposites do not attract as much as birds of a feather flock together. Pain seeks to attach itself to self-pity, and it looks for a victim to supply the venom.

Have you ever wondered why your husband might go to a woman who is a total downgrade from you? Why would he reduce you to this? The truth is he didn't reduce you. He reduced himself. The other woman is broken, incomplete and insecure, and is unable to see that there is something better for her. She'll accept the empty promise that he will leave his wife for her, and won't even consider that in the unlikely event it actually happened, she'd be in danger of losing him in the exact same way.

Often the cheating woman doesn't really want the man to leave his wife for her. If he does, then she becomes the filler of dead space. And while this might be a gut-puncher, married women need to understand that while the other woman may well be better than them in bed, God will never bless that union because it goes against the institution of marriage, which he honors.

Some women want nothing but to encourage everything about your husband that you don't like about him. That allows her to be the opposite of you.

I think it's God working in my soul, but as much as I wanted to expose these other women, I had grace for them. I didn't want people to label them the way the church labeled me.

It's unfair for your spouse to put you in a position where you have to compete for his affection, but she gets what you've cleaned up.

So what is accomplished by getting angry with her? By screaming and yelling? Nothing. If anything she might get a charge out of it. So talk to her. Get to know her. Find out what you need to know.

Of course, at that point you must make it clear to her that she needs to get away and stay away from your husband. You also have to make sure he wants to leave her, because you don't want to be fighting for someone who is reaching for someone else.

The cheating woman can work for your good, or can separate you for good. She is what she is until she allows the broken places within her to become whole. But before you judge the manifestation of an internal unhealthiness, see that the pain of her life attracts the incompleteness in your husband's life. And deal with them both accordingly.

Chapter Five

The Breaking Point

"The truth is, unless you let go, unless you forgive yourself, unless you forgive the situation, unless you realize that the situation is over, you cannot move forward." – Steve Maraboli

This chapter is the one that I fought to write, but I know that it was a much-needed one. All of us in our lives have to come to a place where we desire change.

I remember crying many days on my way to work and/or church, wondering why I was like this. I wanted to be better. I knew this is not who I was but I could not find the path to the answers. I knew that people who sat with me at work and at church were in relationships they knew were not beneficial or productive for their lives. I always knew that I was destined for greatness and that I was born to affect people's lives, but how could I do that in light of my destructive past?

You have read much of my life in this book, but this is the part that almost cost me my life and my children. I will not go into all the details, but the Lord has led me to expose some parts of the story for your benefit. In retrospect I still to this day ask myself how in the world it happened.

My testimony, which I will present in a way that protects certain innocent people, starts when I was part of a ministry in Knoxville, Tennessee. I began to become a part of, as we say, the "inner circle." My position in this ministry began to give me recognition and some administrative pull. Within these years of serving in this ministry, I saw a lot and I heard a lot, but would never reveal what I knew because I was trained that you protect your man and woman of God.

Knowing there is no perfect church or leader, I, like so many others, respected and held our leader in the highest regard.

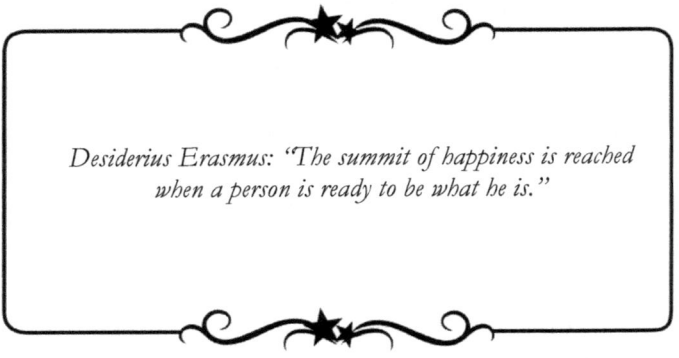

Desiderius Erasmus: "The summit of happiness is reached when a person is ready to be what he is."

After years of serving, our leader decided to file for divorce. It was a dreadful day. I remember clearly that I did not want to go to church that day, because I knew it was not going to be good. A week before that, our leader had called us all into a meeting to inform us of his decision, and we all decided to support and undergird the both of them through this transition, and pray for the healing of both parties.

Some had claimed falsely that our pastor didn't provide for his family. He did, and he was respected for that. Nevertheless, this announcement was devastating and happened at a terrible time. We as a church had just moved into our new multimillion-dollar edifice, and the ministry was very progressive and growing. It was the "happening church" in the city.

So the divorce announcement was a stunner for the congregation, but it hit no one in the way it hit me. I began to hear whispers of an affair between me and the pastor. I was shocked, but I was no stranger to controversy and I recognized that my relationship with him *was* unhealthy. But there it was and there was no changing it.

My approach to the situation didn't help either. My attitude about all the talk was basically: "Oh well, since everybody is talking, let's give them something to talk about."

I knew I was not the reason he left his wife, so I resented all the whispers, but I could have been more of a leader instead of what I did – which was to start functioning as his confidante. I would go to dinner with my pastor so we could talk about the situation. I became his refuge, and that only made my situation worse because I was making myself an even easier target.

The ruthlessness of people surprised me, but maybe it shouldn't have. They were hurting, and rightly or wrongly my behavior was doing little to stem the speculation that I was the other woman. Still, I was surprised by how mean people got, even people I had helped and counseled. People called for my ouster from the church in a public meeting. It became necessary to move my ministry class for college students into my office so they couldn't hear the harsh words coming from the congregation.

At one point I became so upset over the situation that tears came to my eyes during a service, and when I asked an usher for a tissue, she replied, "Over my dead body."
I could not believe I was living this life.

I would oftentimes encourage the pastor to stand strong if this was what he believed he had to do. But was it the right advice? I was like Alice in Wonderland. People started leaving the church, and as rumors rose, the war grew and grew. I remember one day my pastor and I were in my office, having a discussion concerning the truth in a particular passage of Scripture. We were getting a little loud, and as we walked out the office into the hallway, the first lady and I had an altercation. It became very bad, and we were both taken into his office.

From that day, I must admit I did not care who I hurt or who was going to be hurt! I became sick and tired of the church, and I wanted to expose all the information I knew on a whole lot of people. The church started treating my children hatefully, and in people's minds my name had become "HOME WRECKER".

I became like some of the women I talked about in the previous chapter, but I still had a conviction within me that I wrestled with day and night. I was never at peace, but I hid it and portrayed myself as living a life that was not real. I felt as if I had no other choice. I loved this man for what he had taught me. He was my spiritual father. But I did not love him as his wife. As the months went on, I found myself in a web I entangled myself in – another church scandal with a married man.

It broke me.

I remember my son Jamal looking at me with pain in his eyes, tears rolling down his face. He said to me, "AND YOU EXPECT ME TO STILL SERVE YOUR GOD."

It was incredibly hard on my children. No one saw the times when I had to encourage them. No one understood what it was like to have to take my children to school in a car someone had spray-painted, to tell them defiantly, with fire in my bones, "We are going to keep going."

I called my sister and found myself cursing like a sailor. I know I was far from the cross at that moment. And it didn't get better when I got home and called the insurance company to get an estimate on the car damage, which was $4,300. You can't imagine how heated I was at that moment.

And I started scheming. People I had thought were friends were showing themselves to be enemies, and I had a lot of information about these people. I knew their secrets and struggles because I had counseled many of them. I wanted to expose it all, especially when these people started encouraging the pastor to throw me under the bus. The ministry he had built over the course of 20 years was now in jeopardy and people wanted him to make me the scapegoat.

But something inside me knew I should not do it. I was angry and hurt but that wouldn't make it right to violate their confidence, no matter what they were doing now or how I felt about it. So I held my peace.

One month later, my daughter Bre' and I were lying in my bed and heard a noise. Because I lived near the street, I thought a truck had backfired. But when I woke up the next morning, I noticed a huge hole in my door. It was a gunshot. I called the police and they called forensics.

The forensics agent told me he had never seen anything like it. The bullet, he explained, was supposed to go straight and hit my bed. It had to be someone who had been in my house before and knew where my bed was positioned to know where to aim the shot. But the bullet traveled up into the wall, hit a cinder block and fell to the floor.

I called my pastor and told him what had happened, and he came over to the house and talked to the police. I wanted to *fight*. But I realized I had reached the point where I could no longer do this. It was time for me to leave the church.

So did he. He resigned and passed the ministry to his son in the Gospel. I left and begin to attend a primarily Caucasian ministry. I WAS DETERMINED I WAS NOT LEAVING GOD.

That's when I made the mistake of letting my pastor move in with me. He suggested it as a way that he could protect me and my children, which was certainly a concern in the aftermath of the gunshot. It was wrong, but I was angry. So my judgment wasn't what it should have been, nor was it any better some time later when we started to discuss getting married.

Why would I do that? Especially considering the things that were already being said about me? In some ways, that was why I did it. I figured my name was a mess anyway. People hated me then and some of them still hate me to this day, and I believed I was doing myself no good to keep worrying about it.

I considered myself forgiven, both by God and by myself, but at the same time I was in such a deep depression that it led to a nervous breakdown. My baby Bre' would pray over me and ask God to bring my mind back.

I revealed none of this to my pastor, though, as I walked him through his divorce. I didn't know how to break the cycle and I had no one to talk to. I remember running into his soon-to-be-ex-wife in Wal-Mart, and for all my anger, I couldn't fail to recognize just how broken she was. I was grieved as I asked myself the question: "Ane, did you do that?"

Walking out of the store I was more distressed than ever, but I was too far in at this point to back out. Where would he go? What would I do? I couldn't stay in this city, and he had contacted a man of God who was open to helping him relocate and restart his ministry with us – his new family.

Everything was far from OK. We had financial struggles and his other children had been severely affected by the choices he had made. He and I would have arguments, and I began to resent my life. But I didn't blame him. I blamed myself.

So we relocated, together, to Orlando. He began in pastoral leadership in a new church – but even there the scandal followed us because we encountered someone there who had connections to him and knew the history of what had happened.

Our location had changed, but the scars moved with us.

It was hard to see how God was going to get the glory out of this, and after three years of marriage to him the Lord really begin to deal with me and convict me. I really didn't feel a connection with him as his wife, even as I knew that God honors marriage. I asked God to give me a child, and I had a beautiful son. But that did not change the conviction I was feeling that this marriage was not right.

Shortly after the birth of our son, we were sitting together in the living room and I said to him, "You and she are going to get back together. That is your wife."

We had just had a baby and he looked at me with an "Ane, really?" type of look.
But I persisted.
"That woman loves you," I said. "She is connected to you, she loves you".

It was a bizarre argument – almost funny in some respects – but not really.

He hosted a conference in Knoxville, and I went to hear a particular speaker that Saturday morning. He blew me away by saying the following words: "God wants to bless your life, but you have to make your wrong right".

I remember falling out of my seat and screaming. I had never experienced this. That day my life would take a twisted turn. I could not shake the fact that I was looking at people I broke. I understand that we all have choices, and some may say, "Oh, they were using that as an excuse to leave God, or leave the church."

But I didn't want to be the source of that excuse. I felt badly. I was carrying a burden I could not remove. I could not pray this off, I could not fast this off, and I could not counsel this off. I simply had to make my wrong *right*.

I then developed this motto: Do what is right versus doing what is easy. So that year I was invited to attend a gathering at a church in Jacksonville, Florida. I went, and the man's message was so powerful I literally cried the entire 45 minutes. He ministered to women about having relationships with their leaders, and taught that you cannot turn a daughter into a wife.

"Your congregation embraces her as their sister, and they treat her like their sister," he said "When you transition her, you cannot expect the people to transition with you, and that is why it affects the church like that. That's your daughter!"

I ran to my car after church and I wept. I called my friend Myra and said, "I have messed up my life."
She talked to me all the way home.

I said, "What are people going to think about me?"

I got home and sat in my car and read the story of Bathsheba three times, and when I researched her name it meant "daughter".

I repented and asked God how I was going to make this right. We had a *gorgeous* home and cars and ministry, but I had hurt this woman!

Three weeks later, I was invited to attend a women's meeting. The facilitator's name was Johnnie Mae Swinson. She called me up for prayer and said, "Young lady, look at me. You will be somebody great one day. God has some awesome things for your life. But you have to get yourself together and allow God to heal your life. Don't allow your issues to destroy you."
She did not know the mental battle that I was in because of my new decision to do right. Everything felt so wrong.

I went into the house told my husband we needed to talk. Men hate to hear these four words. I sat him down and explained I didn't know what we had to do, but we couldn't stay married. I was his spiritual daughter. He was supposed to be with her. *That's your wife.* We got into this huge debate about God honoring marriage.

My sisters, I cannot explain it all. I knew they were supposed to be together. I would then pray and ask God to heal her, and someday allow me to apologize to her for what I did.

Nobody else mattered. I knew that I was set apart by God, but I did not want to be ministering and empowering women all over the world while my conscience weighed on me about how I left this woman broken – a woman who had been nothing but nice to me and my children.

In August, I was invited to go on the Word Network. In front of 87 million people, I proceeded to share my life. There was no mistaking that deer-in-the-headlight stare. I felt the whole room change, and I thought to myself, "I am so afraid. What in the world have I done?"

I then knew this was my right of passage to encourage women like me! My office phone rang off the hook. We were flooded with testimonies and calls from women and men who were now in this type of relationship.

One particular one made me exhale. He asked to speak to me when he called my office. I did not talk to everybody but I just felt compelled to speak with him, and he said to me while crying, "Ma'am, when I was eighteen my mother had an affair with our pastor, she got pregnant and when it came out he denied it, she had the baby but the pressure was too much for her that she hung herself, and I was left to raise my brother. I have not been back to church since. I am now 32."

He then said, "Thank you, I feel like you were my mother's redemption, thank you, thank you, thank you, tonight I forgave him."

That was worth it all. I received many calls like this. Leaders called me crying, asking for prayer. First ladies called me. It was such a powerful experience – I knew it was time to make my wrong right.

I was walking through the airport and called my ex-husband and asked to speak to her. I apologized to her. I told her I was sorry for hurting her. I messed up her life, her money. I broke her children. I destroyed her church. I was broken but thankful I was given the opportunity to say FORGIVE ME.

She accepted my apology and encouraged me! That was a miracle, and I was so humbled and thankful.

My issue took this woman's life and broke this man's

stride. Many will say it took two, of course, but I am taking responsibility for my part. You will never heal what you fail to confront! I then asked God to heal my life and heal me. It was no longer about who I was becoming. I was sick of myself. It was months after I realized what I had to do that we separated and got a divorce. I knew I had to release him. It was hard because now people were affected again, and thinking about it is overwhelming.

My son, who was three at the time, would miss his dad and not understand why his daddy was not at home anymore. His father made the decision to move back to Knoxville to reestablish his ministry. But he also got the most beautiful blessing out of all of this: He REMARRIED his wife.

My son goes every holiday and summer to Knoxville, and spends time with his father. She does not show him any partiality, she treats him like her child, and I appreciate that. I do not know if she has mental struggles, but she never shows it.

My sisters, it was not worth seeing the pain that I caused. It has not been easy but I am now so determined by the grace of God to never go back again. I allowed myself to know who I really am. I had to face some nasty things about me, but it was necessary for me in order to love myself and love someone else. I was a wreck. I needed to be in a process of healing, and I am learning that healing is an everyday process. We learn something new about who we are.

My evolution has been amazing. Learning me has been hard and fun. I discovered that under all of those insecurities there is an *amazing* person. The most heartbreaking thing was that I realized when you are in your trial, you lose people – a lot of people. Even with their dysfunctions they do not want to be connected to anything that they perceive is a failure. They misinterpret your course, become chameleons and change like the weather.

Even now, traveling and meeting new people, I find

that some are telling other ministers' wives to watch me because of my past. That pierces my heart, but I have to be prepared for the worst from anybody. I can see why they leave, and they were not called to my trial with me, but it's impossible to know who or what to trust.

People will label you, but God does not restrict you to those labels. His plan for our lives is so GREAT. His thoughts about me come from His Grace toward me. Man's opinion does not abort your promise. If anyone does, YOU DO!

I was determined to find out what mine would be. It is sprouting into a well of wealth. I am whole and happy, I love me even on a bad day. When I am having an off day, I refuse to return to the place that broke me. I keep going, I empower myself, I pray, I call my positive friends and I keep it moving. I am certainly not saying that it is always easy. *No ma'am.* But the benefits that are attached to me are worth it. My breaking point was when I hurt someone in a major way. If that does not pull at your heart, then something is wrong with your person! I read this quote, and it helps me on many days to get through my moments of being alone.

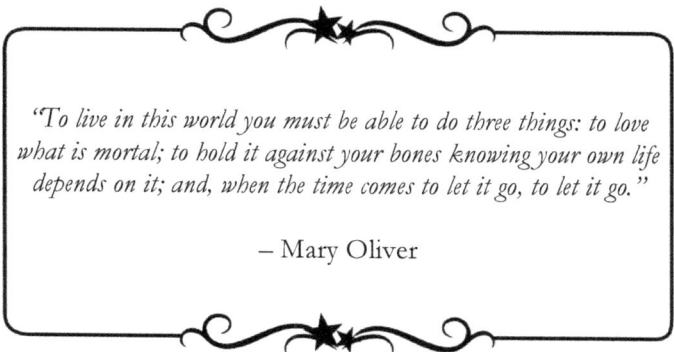

"To live in this world you must be able to do three things: to love what is mortal; to hold it against your bones knowing your own life depends on it; and, when the time comes to let it go, to let it go."

– Mary Oliver

As I started my new life as a single pastor, I should have used more wisdom. Because I didn't, I caused some pain for my people. I began dating six months after my divorce – a younger man – and it caused major confusion amongst the congregation. I felt like I couldn't win for losing, but we live in a judgmental world and I wasn't making all the right moves to prove to people that I had changed.

My sister, life has a way of answering you back. I wanted some better answers! It has been hard trying to rebuild my name, trying to prove to people that I am changed. But you cannot change people's view of you, so you have to just keep living, and your character will prove you! I used to live life thinking, "Will I ever know what love is? Will I ever experience dating a single man and really being complete? Will I know how to function as his prize and not being a secret?"

Now, my life would be controlled by fears of being single and waiting for my jewel to find me. I was afraid that if I did date someone else, they would find out about my past as much as I tried to protect it. It was out, even in Jacksonville. People still shunned me, but I had to be all right with that. God gave me some special people in my life and I love them so much!

I'm tearing up telling you about it.

There were moments when I did not think that I was going to make it, and I had to encourage myself that I would. I began dating again and it was hard. I found myself scared of commitment, and sisters, please listen to this: I was single but still a secret. I found myself again in a new relationship, but the same spirit was there. I finally understood that if I did not change my standard, this would be my pattern.

I removed myself from that relationship, and it was some months later that my now-husband called me and wanted to meet me at Starbucks. I refused at first because I did not want to deal with this rollercoaster ride any longer. I was redefining myself. But I ended up going and I am so happy that I did.

He asked me to date him for three months and then marry him. I had to know what I deserved, and I was beginning to live as such. I was no longer desperate. I just wanted a whole committed relationship, and I was not playing second anymore!

This may get me hated, but stand in line. I really want to take this moment right here to say this to my sisters who are in the church because that's where I fell. Just because you are in the church does not exempt you. We see and hear of developments of leaders becoming involved with "groupies" or with their members who desire to have one night with the king all the time.

I have turned down invitations to room invites, opportunities to be the other woman. I have heard reported cases of rape, and even the alleged use of drugs and alcohol. Why did I expose this in this season?

You do not need to be the hand that rocks that cradle. Many will not agree with me, but if you walk into this trap with a pastor, understand while he is a man and he has issues as well, he will come out of it better than you will. He will be ministered to, supported and undergirded with financial backing. His wife will have other women who will draw to her.

You? You will be fifth to none. And this is a war that you cannot fight alone. Before you decide to cross the line in the sand, look at his legacy. It takes one to flirt but two to make a decision to fall.

Don't put yourself in a counseling session without his wife, or counsel with a female leader. Before you consider crossing that line, look in her eyes. Look at his children. Be a woman. Do not force yourself into his circle you probably cannot handle it.

I cannot express this strongly enough. I have experienced and witnessed, behind closed doors, this illicit and selfish behavior. There are many women who fall prey to and/or pursue men, and have been surprised that they could not handle the pressure.

It's almost like you sign a secret contract. Some of the men will even have the attitude, "If you tell, they won't believe you. Look who I am. It will be your loss".

So this is not to make the man look bad. It is to shake my sisters' thinking. I have been here and I have walked some of this. I know women who have walked it in other ways. We got out and so can you, and if you are contemplating it, remember that you only see through the eyes of your own desires!

Also understand that you will not stop you if your needy places are being comforted. The charisma, the glamour and the glitz, his fresh dress, his lifestyle, his ability to command and look out for you, being the one he will be calling after the fact, but . . . IT IS STILL NOT WORTH YOUR DIGNITY. You deserve more.

THE MONEY EXCHANGE IS STILL NOT WORTH IT.

After I became a big girl, I wanted to explore something new and out of the box. I had a really cool best friend, and surprisingly we had started dating and hit it off, but because we were not sure if this was what we wanted to make permanent – he was younger and I was older – we had our reservations. We thought, "Oh boy, what are people going to say now?"

Nevertheless, WE LOVED IT. We offered each other what we had never experienced, it worked for us.
But what I thought would be a celebrated occasion was a nightmare. His family totally rejected our union. So I found myself in another scandal, but this time I was labeled a "COUGAR".

I was doing what men have been doing for years. It was refreshing and I was loving it, but I felt like I was losing because people did not agree. He, on the other hand, was sure. And in spite of the controversy I knew this time it was right.

I am learning that people will be people. Sisters, my breaking points have served as life lessons for me. And in my new marriage, for which I am so grateful, it paid off. I am married to a gentleman. He is adorable and strong. He is a leader and he protects and takes care of our family. He has never judged my past. He loves me and that's all that matters.

I am married to my best friend. He is my buddy, and you can have the same thing. He pushes me to be greater! So, with that, I am over people and their views of me. There are people who are assigned to your NOW, so *free yourself* and live your life.

Not long ago I was walking down the street in Las Vegas, singing a song by Faith Evans: *"If I had to do it all again, I looked to the sky and said, Lord thank you for all of that"*.

Your breaking point may not be like mine, but we all have one, and when it happens do not miss your opportunity for transformation. When I began to heal me, and identify who I was through God's eyes, I began to bloom into who I am today. Sister, bloom and move forward!

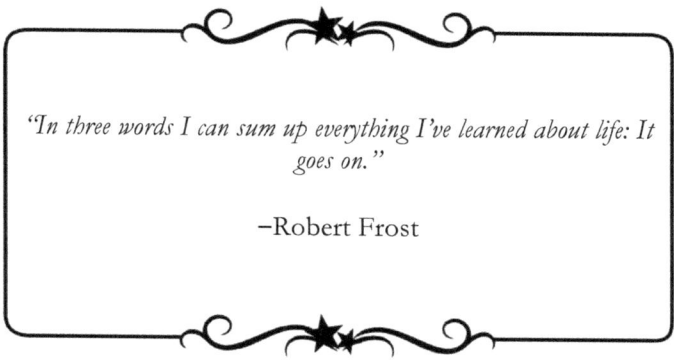

"In three words I can sum up everything I've learned about life: It goes on."

–Robert Frost

Chapter Six

Through the Eyes of the Other Woman

Let me offer you a different perspective on the "Other Woman." It's not the view you often hear, which warns of her as the Jezebel spirit in the church who is out to take your man and bring down the ministry. I'm not saying those things couldn't be true. I'm just saying that's not the whole story.

I have sat in many conferences, at lunch tables, at dinner socials – or listened to radio and TV shows – where no one really addresses this issue quite right. Everyone knows how to address the *act* of adultery. It's easy to judge and condemn the act. But it's much more difficult to address what leads to it.

I'll never forget the church service in which I heard a woman get up and give her testimony of how the Lord had healed her marriage. It was filled with statements about how, when the spirit comes into your midst that would bring temptation to adultery, you have to learn how to kill it. The people in the congregation roared with applause. They were high-fiving each other.

I just sort of smiled as I watched this. I respected her process, but to me whatever healing she'd experienced seemed tinged with bitterness. I decided it was time for me to take the podium.

Needless to say, the atmosphere in the room changed quite a bit when I opened by explaining to them exactly what my experience had been:

"Well," I told them, "I am the surviving other woman. I represent the ones that y'all want to kill."

The room became utterly silent. The tension was strong. I didn't care. If nothing else, I had their attention! And I held it for 45 minutes straight, telling them all about my journey and how my life and my struggle had become an open book. I challenged them to let me speak truly and honestly with them, because I wonder sometimes if people really want honesty.

The truth, I told them, is that no one can really take your mate from you unless there is first access to him. And there is never going to be access unless you let it happen. A man may celebrate your birthday and anniversary, and he may hold your hand in public, but that doesn't mean there is nothing inside of him that you're failing to speak to. It doesn't mean there is no pain, void, insecurity, fear, hurt or lack of fulfillment. And you can't necessarily put it on your man to tell you about it. He may not even know how to put words to what he's missing. You're his wife! You're supposed to feel out his needs. It's supposed to be a priority to you.

None of this excuses adultery. But I'm not talking about excusing. I'm talking about knowing how and why it happens. Men are processors, and they have to work things through in their own minds. Then, if they do manage to identify what's going on, they have to be confident their wives are willing to receive what they're telling them openly.

Would you? *Are you sure?* Would you take him seriously and make him feel like you're glad he told you? Would you act on what he told you? Because you can talk all you want about killing the predator, but if you don't address the reasons she had access in the first place, why should you think another one won't get the same opportunity?

People say they want the truth, but I don't think they really want to confront it all that often. Often they hide behind religious activities like prayer and fasting – both of which I believe in and practice, by the way – as a substitute for really sitting and down and honestly talking about what's going on. You need to do the one without neglecting the other. Otherwise you're wasting your time talking about the whore or Jezebel or whatever you want to call her. Hating her doesn't really solve your problem.

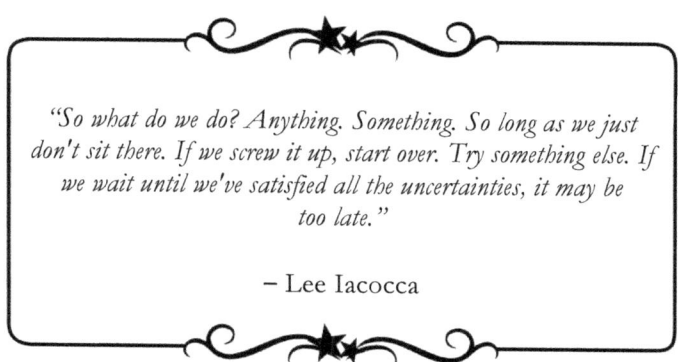

"So what do we do? Anything. Something. So long as we just don't sit there. If we screw it up, start over. Try something else. If we wait until we've satisfied all the uncertainties, it may be too late."

– Lee Iacocca

I know you feel violated, disrespected and deceived – because you are and you were! But believe it or not, God wants to give her a chance to live again. She still has His gifts. She still has a purpose that He's given her. And she's going to pay a price for disrupting your life, but it's going to be up to God what that price will be.

When I found out it was happening to me, I went off. Completely off. I would have ripped her to shreds if I'd had the opportunity. I wanted others to feel the sense of betrayal and join me in my crusade to destroy this woman.

But what was I doing? I was reliving this experience from the other side. And ultimately, in my heart, I did not want to expose her. I didn't want her to feel the ostracism I had felt.

Emotionally women always want to view the issue primarily as a violation by another woman. We may deal with the man privately, but publicly she's the one who's going to get our scorn. She invaded your territory. She's the enemy.

The last thing you'd consider is protecting her. But you're not going to help in the healing of your marriage by seeking to wound her or humiliate her. And after the fighting, yelling, threats and tears, you can't make him leave her. He has to be willing. He has to want to deal with himself and his own issues – and close the access.

She is a woman just like you. Every woman that gets into an affair is not a whore. Some are. Some delight in the challenge. Some are rude and disrespectful. But the access had to come from somewhere. Couples need to find out what happened, because before there was a you, there was a road to this. It just did not start with a hello from another woman.

Once you realize that cheating was and is his choice, no matter how bad the marriage is, it should prompt some serious communication. And not just between you and him. I remember having a conversation with a woman who cheated with my partner – being so angry, but at the same time having a certain peace because I could not allow myself to go back to the old ways by lashing out.

I warned that heifer that she had picked the wrong person to mess with, but I also told her: I used to be you. I am the author to women like you. *So you just played yourself.*

And once I got over the intense desire to whoop this woman from one side of the street down to the other, I started asking myself the inevitable questions. Did this happen because of me? Did I push him to her? Was I pretty enough? All kinds of questions like this flooded my mind. I was yelling at myself as much as I was yelling at her. These questions became the haunted house of my mind.

I would hold it together because I could not allow anyone to know what was going on, and because I needed to protect my image and his name. But finally, after weeks and months of torment, I realized through counseling that no one does anything unless they choose to. I had to take my mind back, pull my emotions together and deal with the shock of this shift in me. I could not allow it to rule my judgment. I still had to move forward and get out of this unhealthy place.

And I had to ask myself questions that I never thought that I would have to ask:

1. Do I love him enough to make this work?
2. Am I willing to forgive and forget?
3. Can I allow grace to be my reason of reconciliation?
4. Can I stay in this and not allow it to force me into a picture instead of true rebuilding?
5. Am I strong enough within myself and God to stick this out?
6. Is it worth me trusting this again?

Trust has always been extremely important to me, and I found myself not trusting anything that came out of his mouth. I remember one time watching him minister and thinking to myself, *he's probably lying*! He turned to me and said, "Ane, the Lord gave me a word for you."
My response was, "Hold it." Because I would not receive it. Not through him.

Finally, I had to reshape my thinking. I had to choose to be real with myself and ask myself what in this was my lesson to empowerment and growth?

What had happened was not my responsibility, but I knew I had to create an opportunity for the failure of this man to be covered and restored, whether he wanted that with or without me. I had to separate the act from the reality. I had to be willing to be open and honest. Most women will say that their relationship was perfect until *she* came along. That's not true, if it wasn't that woman, it would have been another one or something else.

I have witnessed true healing and growth in couples who talk and heal for real. It is a painful process, but you have to be willing to stay in prayer and understand that if you choose to stay in this, you have to choose to walk free. You will not leave this unlearned.

Can I give you a bit of wisdom? This may not have been about him, and sometimes God uses strange things to get your attention because you were too comfortable and did not see the signs of better until you were in pain for a purpose. If God allowed you to face this, His purpose is to turn it good! You have to deal with the disappointment of your ideal being tainted.

Remember, with this choice you have a road to sojourn! It may have been a dormant issue that was never really rooted up. You can try to hide from the other woman – just get her out – thinking that the problem will go away. No, it will not. There were signs before she came. You just failed to recognize them – or refused to.

This road to reconciliation will not be easy but it can be worth the fight. There are times when the marriage will not survive the affair, but the other woman did not do it alone. Face that. It was not a forced entrance. One way or another she was invited. If you are the cheating woman or have been cheated on, please deal honestly and thoroughly in order to get positive results.

By the way, it's nonsense when we say, "Women are attracted to men in authority." Not all women fit that description by any means, and we have to stop categorizing our sisters in the same pot. Women love security – both temporary and permanent – and we need the power of protection. It makes us feel like we can rest if we have a man in our lives that can offer a support that makes us feel secure. Remember, at the end of the day, she is still a woman. She is a cycle of an unprocessed seed that is in her

– one that she has not been willing to heal.

We treat this fact like it's a secret, but the way we live reveals it openly. And when the bottom falls, we lose our ground to stand on. It knocks the wind out of our being and snaps us into this life of revenge. It is amazing how you can be so poised, but when violated you become violent. That's when you realize you are not as put together as you think. Marriage is a forever place of revealing and healing. It takes accountability, feeling safe again, feeling protected and a priority again. It should be, and ultimately can become, a garden of *safety*.

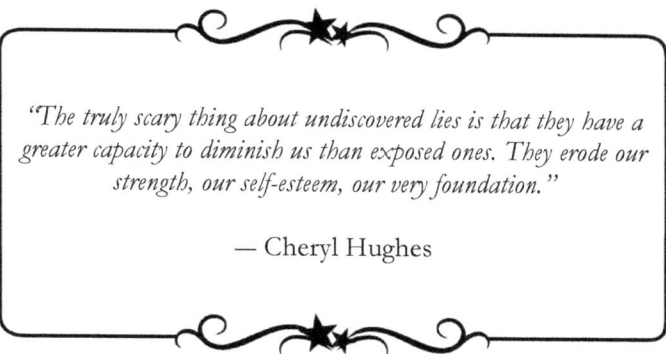

"The truly scary thing about undiscovered lies is that they have a greater capacity to diminish us than exposed ones. They erode our strength, our self-esteem, our very foundation."

— Cheryl Hughes

It is your decision to live again. And everything you have to do in order to make it happen is also your decision. You can decide to live *better* instead of living *bitter*. You can get over the fear that he is being dishonest with you, or still talking to another woman, or still cheating on you. You can get over viewing yourself with derision. You can stop being ruled by what you think other people are saying.

It's a matter of stopping and taking control of your mind.

I had to take this pain to God so that I would not live within the walls of this deception. I remember getting mad at God because He was not moving fast enough to get this hell out of my heart, out of mind, out of our relationship.

But guess what: I had to realize I am not in control of God's timing for healing. I wanted God to kill him, or her, or both of them. I hated this, and I had to be challenged to move on in my life.

My history is not my destiny, and I had to embrace that! It was one of my greatest teachers of how to become a more powerful woman, and speaking him into becoming a more powerful man.

Now understand: You cannot make a boy a man, so if your spouse is not willing to grow and he remains determined to live in an immoral fashion, that is not license for you to make people pay, or to fulfill a payback, or to take the focus off of him. You need to make a choice to heal *you*. You are that valuable.

Growth can sometimes be hidden in the most uncropped fields. We always look for perfect grass to cut, and your process to self-discovery is to learn how to desire to crop a field that looks dry and unturned. I have learned quickly that a dry field just needs to be watered. It needs more attention. But seeds can still be planted in the soil.

Your marriage right now may be a dry ground. Water it again. Plant new seeds by planting a new you. Do not lie to yourself: It will take work. Take a chance. You may nervously ask, *what if it doesn't work?*

My response: What if it does?

There's a fairy-tale, simple way of living that exempts you from the trials that sharpen us for better. The first step in healing your heart is understanding that is a fairy tale. Your heart does not have to stay broken. This is between you and your spouse, and you will choose how far your relationship will go. Will it survive just enough to restore and hold together your image? Or will it truly begin to reveal the love and true meaning of what brought you together in the beginning?

Ask yourself, can I live this life without him? There is nothing wrong with loving your man back to life. You cannot be indebted to the love you have, and not to the struggles you've endured.

Every three months you should have a Straight Talk Day, and on that day, ask your spouse three words: "Are We Good?"

Talk openly with no holds barred. You choose what you will tell. The way you set the standards for your relationship is the way the two of you will live it. It is easy to give up and walk away, but before you do, do some soul-searching and pull your spouse away from your everyday environment. And invite him: Let's talk about us. Let's look over our year and see what can we do better.

You do not have to live in fear that this will happen again. Do not allow this pain to rule your relationship. Rehearse to yourself: IT IS NEVER TOO LATE TO BEGIN AGAIN.
God is the God of fresh starts and new beginnings.

If your spouse refuses to participate, then you move forward and progress. And maybe you'll have the chance to reach back and heal another sister with your story. Your pain was not and will not be wasted.

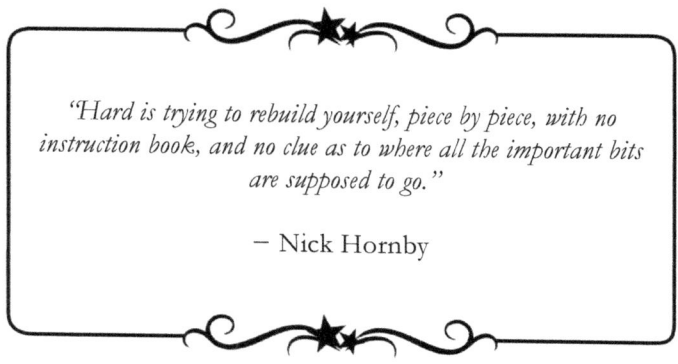

"Hard is trying to rebuild yourself, piece by piece, with no instruction book, and no clue as to where all the important bits are supposed to go."

– Nick Hornby

Chapter Seven

The Recovery

"Always put yourself in the other person's shoes; if it hurts you it probably hurts them too." –Anonymous

Life Is Really Not a Fairy Tale

I just wanted to end this journey by applauding your decision to make a life change. You are too powerful, fabulous and innovative to play the role of someone who already has it. Step back, reevaluate your purpose, regain momentum and take your life back.

Take back who you lost, revamp your standards, and get it together. I would be lying to you if I said that it would be easy or that it would take you just one day to be better. The truth is, it will take you one day at a time, but you can do it and you can live a life that is free.

I remember asking God to give me Ane back. I wanted to become the woman that He purposed me to become.

Now, I thank God that He has blessed my life with a beautiful husband — we are honest with each other. My life is not perfect but it is happy!

My relationship with my mother is good. I had to ask God to heal my heart of the anger that I held. I had to accept that she did the best she knew how and I value her for that. I realize she may not have been perfect but she was assigned to me and I appreciate her sacrifice to be my mom and raise me.

Although my relationship with my biological father is not healed, I have been blessed with some remarkable men — one on the East Coast and one on the West Coast — who are my surrogate dads.

I was blessed to have a spiritual mentor as a father figure as well to force me into staying free. He was HARD on me but I needed it.

Sometimes you have to take the good with the bad, smile with the sad, love what you've got, and remember what you had. Learn to forgive, but never forget, learn from your mistakes, but never regret, people change, things go wrong, but just remember, life goes on.

– Unknown

When you are walking out of a cycle you will need someone in your life to be honest with you and about you. I had to stop blaming others and becoming upset because I didn't have a role model as a child or anyone to be there for me. I had to stop shifting the blame and move on.

Your mom or your dad may not have been there to celebrate, but they gave you life to make it happen. There are many opportunities waiting for you, so arise, fight, and be determined to be successful. Take the limits off and do you, girl, there are a pool of sisters cheerleading you to your abundance!

You are my FANTABULOUS sister! Remember, you have the goods to make the right man a wonderful wife. You have so many untapped avenues in you that can only be touched by YOUR man; the one God will bless you with.

There is no perfect man, but there will be one that is perfect for you. I believe every man has the power to evoke his woman into her passion for life, so when you avail yourself, there is a man waiting on his princess. He is ready to push you, to support you, love and accept you.

I have come through a lot and I have had to conquer many issues and through God all things are possible if you believe. I am a better person than I was and I can encourage many of you to turn your focus inwardly and evaluate yourself. Ask yourself the question: who is the one that you see and do you like her? I had to take that step one day. I poured my heart out to my best friend and she gave me a path to healing:

1. Identify what made you go here
2. Be honest about your heart
3. Accept your responsibility
4. Respect yourself again
5. Build the woman in you and love you
6. Get out
7. Stay Out

I would call her when I was struggling and she would encourage me. I was crawling and then when I began to take steps, I progressed and I knew I wanted to be a man's dream girl and not his benefit plan. I made it, so can you.

Take your life back and live . . . I DID!

"The rate at which a person can mature is directly proportional to the embarrassment he can tolerate.

– Douglas Engelbart

Chapter Eight

A Better Way Forward

"If God closes a door AND a window, consider the fact that it might be time to build a whole new house." —Mandy Hale

The Single Woman

Before I close out this journey, I want to have a heart to heart with my single sisters. Imagine we are in a room alone, just you and I. Get a pillow, a cup of java and let's have girl talk for real. I want to give it to you straight.

First, we tell ourselves lies about our relationships when they are or have consumed our ability to have healthy judgments concerning our decisions. We conjure up excuses to validate our reason to be accessible and have guiltless feelings to our false impressions of real love.

I want to ask you a question, because we're talking, right? It's just you and me: If the relationship is so beneficial to you, why does it have to be secret and why is it so emotionally draining? We sketch images of make-believe reality structures which are only right between you and your lover.

If you cannot be truthful with yourself, find someone who has the toughness and the compassion to be honest with you. There is someone who has been assigned to you – my advice is to confide in someone who will not be ashamed to be your friend, confidant or mentor while you are walking through your process.

I have learned we all need somebody who will not kick us further than we are but will let us stand on their shoulders until we get strong again. That takes a special someone. My sister, I am convinced that most people never recover because of these three keys:

Key #1
They fail to listen

Key #2
They are sorry just because they got caught, not because they want to change

Key #3
They seek advice from the wrong people

You need to know if the only advice you hear is from yourself, you will make stupid decisions, and if you are the smartest person in your circle, then you need to drop that circle until you can be effective again.

God will put people in your path who simply do not care about your past, only where you go from here. Know that the situation made you, it is making you, it promoted you and it can develop you. Let it stop there because YOU HAVE NOTHING TO PROVE TO ANYBODY, and live to complete your purpose.

Now, when someone is put in your life to be your coach and friend, respect their willingness to believe in you.

You will never be perfect but you can be mature – stop allowing yourself to have time limits and don't put your life on hold!

Women, we are CRAZY! We are very emotional and our hormones have us in all kinds of extremes: we go from menstrual cycles, PMS, post-partum depression and menopause; we go from hot to cold, cold to hot; it appears that God made us fickle; we get agitated, aggravated, we want to kick the dog, cat, scream at the kids, throw the dishes and then turn around and cook and be sweet! We are unique individuals. My, my, if a man can handle more than one of us, he is somebody!!! I really do not know how he does it.

I would be depriving you of truth if I told you that it was easy being single but it does pay off, if you wait well you will be paid back well. You will be what you stand for! Some sweetheart of a man will love you and be excited about having you.

When I was single I used to attend conferences, and it would usually turn out like this: women lecturing to women that were either married all their adult life, or someone who had never been married basically telling me to minister to myself.

I needed to experience progression. I needed advanced wisdom – someone who could make some sense out of this madness going on in my life. Instead, I would get suggestions like:

"Look at yourself in the mirror and tell yourself that you are beautiful." (I did.)
"Take yourself out to dinner." (I did.)
"Take a bubble bath, listen to some music and love on yourself." (I did.)
"Take yourself to the movies." (I did.)
"Go get your sister and be accountable and empower each other." (I did.)

And it worked for a season – a very short one – but I wanted a fine man in my presence. I desired a voice with some bass in it.

After a while we would be crying together and one would be strong one day and the other would be weak; we held on and eventually we became sick of looking at each other. I wanted to smell some cologne. I wanted to wear my sexy and pretty pajamas for my man and not another girls' sleepover.

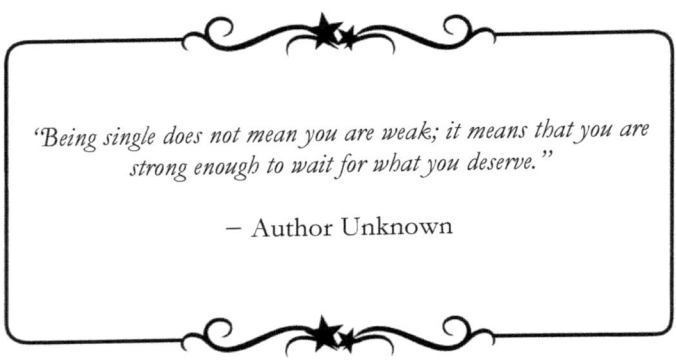

"Being single does not mean you are weak; it means that you are strong enough to wait for what you deserve."

– Author Unknown

The Married Woman

If you are married, pay attention:

Take the time to heal, relearn, rebuild, regain your sexy and talk to your husband. Take down your defenses and fight like a girl. Put the "wanna do" back into it. Identify where you can change and where you can be better and ask yourself a question: *Did I do anything to shut my man down or push my man away?* Are you roommates or married?

Now, if he has a problem and just will not be faithful that is one thing on its own, but if you have a good man, evaluate the problem, get counseling, take your marriage back and live in it. You were made to fit him and with him, please do not allow another woman to come in and wreck what you and your husband have built together! You are, and have been, the strength of that man. If he does walk away, you know you gave it your best.

- Never allow your communication to become silent, never nag him until he begins to feel as if he is your child and not your husband. Learn when to respond and learn how to be quiet.
- Govern your responses and know when to interject your opinion because sometimes he just needs you to listen to his pressure.
- Learn how to fight fair and don't throw his mistakes or shortcomings in his face.
- Stop trying to prove to him that you can be more of a man than he is.
- Learn to be each other's friend.
- Never allow money to divide you; establish who is better with the money and handle it.
- Be honest about your places of insecurity. Tell your husband when you do not feel secure or when you do not feel safe in his love.
- Give him positive affirmation; let him know that you appreciate his ability to do his best in taking care of the family.
- Take the time to be involved in each other's day.
- Speak affirmations to each other.
- Guard his weakness and stop telling your friends and family when you are angry with your spouse.
- Don't push him to have options, making statements like: "I don't need you", "I can do this without you", or "What do I need you for if I am handling everything?"
- Make sure you don't make him feel as if he is your pimp or ATM machine; know that he wants to take care of you.
- Keep your passion exciting, keep him pursuing you,

and keep him interested.
Remember the three "b's":
1. Work your BUDGET together
2. Work your BODY into his mind
3. Have his BACK always protect him good, bad and indifferent

Throw a curve ball in his life: if you have a man that has an office and he works all the time, go to him, put his favorite drink on the desk, kiss him and whisper in his ear. Let him know you don't have any panties on and walk out, then count to 10. Watch how quickly he will come running and if he does not come running we have problem.

While driving in the car put on the song that you both love, go back down memory lane, reach over and start kissing and touching on him. The car will either be pulled over or he will rush home. If he pushes you away we still have a problem.

Be creative: make him think that you have gone insane, get some sexy lingerie, romance him, make love to his mind, and love your marriage back to life. Ask him what his fantasy is and take him on the ride of his life.

Take him on a walk in the park, have a picnic and create an outdoor oasis of heaven. Massage his shoulders, ask him about his day, tell him about your day, enjoy your husband, enjoy growing again. I have learned to give up my right to be right at times and it does not make me less of a woman. I promise you, marriage can still work.

When your husband recognizes that he has hurt you, a good man will heal you back to his heart! If you stayed with your man through hell, I stand and applaud you. You are not stupid, and you proved that it was worth standing for.

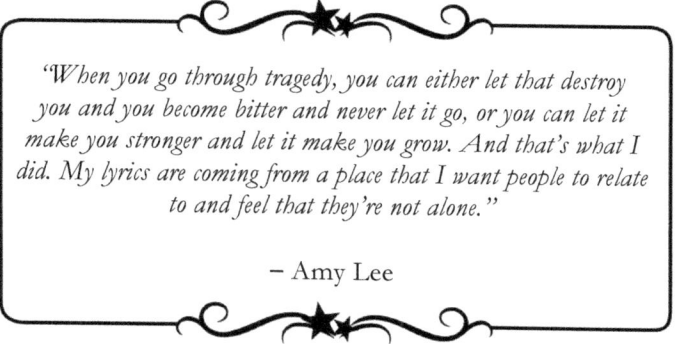

"When you go through tragedy, you can either let that destroy you and you become bitter and never let it go, or you can let it make you stronger and let it make you grow. And that's what I did. My lyrics are coming from a place that I want people to relate to and feel that they're not alone."

– Amy Lee

A Message to the Man . . .

Love your wife. If you have experienced infidelity or if you are contemplating it, *do not do it, it is not worth it.* You are the protector of your wife's heart, the man who holds her insecurities. She looks to you for guidance and security; to break your wife you're opening her up to many facets of insecurities. That is devastating.

It is embarrassing and it creates mental torments in her emotions. If this is you, heal your wife, pull her close and restore what has been broken. Trust has been shattered and it may take her some time, but a strong woman will stay there with you. She may give you hell privately but she will be your force publicly. She will honor you and her family.

If you have a good woman, appreciate her. She may not be perfect but she works well with you. If you have invested a lot into your home and family don't risk it on someone who does not know you. Your wife has been given the grace to handle you, and you have a command from God to love her the way Christ loved the church and gave Himself for it.

It is not easy to reconnect with your spouse, but it will be worth it if you give it a chance. Go get your wife back and make her your girlfriend again! Close the breach, open your emotions and take your marriage back. Do not allow any other female to know that you are discontented in your marriage because this opens up doors, and inquisitiveness is not good for a broken man.

Your wife has the capacity to breed what you need from her — give to her straight and she will meet the expectation if she can. If she can't, try to always create a place to make her know that you love her and because men love from production, you show us you love us by the way you provide. That is GREAT, but get to know the heart of your wife, attempt to seek for an understanding instead of being understood. Take the time to communicate with her.

Thank you for listening, now go get your wife, give her a hug and ask her if the two of you can build a more intimate relationship and begin again, and if you choose to walk away please give your family the respect and do it with dignity. Either way it will still be painful because separation hurts everyone, it divides everything.

I know you may not "be in love" with her anymore and if that is the case, if you are certain that it cannot be restored, still guard her and protect your life. It is a hard road to recovery, it is not impossible, but save yourself the scrutiny. Just don't walk away: talk to your children and consider every facet of your decision. Remember, YOU ARE SOMEONE'S HERO.

You know it takes a special woman to handle your ex-life, when your children come and spend time with you; the talks of how your family used to be . . . re-visiting family vacations and holidays; to questions like, "How did you and my mom get together?"

It will all come up because this life is more than thrills, and hips, it's a juggling act! But if you still love her, in the words of Al Green: *Let's Stay Together.*

Life happens, mistakes take place, go do it, you can still make it happen, she is waiting for you to tell her she is worth the fight for your marriage. From one sister to her brother, you have what it takes to make her heart dance to your music again. You are her greatest lyric, so get it together, be honest, forgive, heal, let go and bring reformation to your house.

"Always remember that a perfect relationship is built on compromises and a great deal of give and take on both sides. When you fall in love with a person appreciate their uniqueness rather than comparing them to the image of your dream lover. Learn to adjust to each other's habits, instead of trying to change each other to fit your requirements."

– Unknown Author

CHAPTER NINE
One-on-One Accountability

For me to deal with these struggles and patterns of behavior, I needed to find another woman I could talk to. But it couldn't be just anyone. It had to be someone I respected, who would not be threatened by my strong personality – someone who could see my gentleness and my deep desire to change. I needed to be able to tell her the truth.

But even more so, I had to tell myself the truth. Relationships are almost like anthropology insofar as women of all nationalities have one thing in common – they all want to be loved, respected and safely secured in a man's heart.

Or so I thought! Was I wrong? I kept wondering why relationships always end up so much more complicated than that. My fantasy of making my man the center of my world and receiving that type of love never quite played out as I hoped. Even a person who touches you so profoundly in a given moment may not give you quite the idyllic life you're looking for – and while no one sets out to damage the other, damage still occurs.

Was I looking for something that just couldn't exist? I needed to deal with that question honestly, or the best talking partner in the world wouldn't be able to help me.

That accountability could have helped prevent me from going down a very unwise road – one in which I made the entire measurement of my womanhood about being loved by a man. There is nothing at all wrong with being loved by a man, of course, but when that's the only way you measure who you are, guess what happens:

That man has power over you, and you don't want that. You want to be necessary, not needy. You want to be able to give love, and you want to know how to handle the receiving of love. That only happens when you're a confident person in your own right.

"I, with a deeper instinct, choose a man who compels my strength, who makes enormous demands on me, who does not doubt my courage or my toughness, who does not believe me naive or innocent, who has the courage to treat me like a woman."

– Anais Nin

When I've been able to share my experiences and my struggles with a strong woman in that one-on-one setting, the insight I receive is a serious reality check. She doesn't just see me through the man's eyes. She sees me through eyes that understand my perspective. Her experiences are much the same as my own. And because I'm not obsessed with winning (or keeping) her heart, she and I can be honest with each other in a way that it's much more difficult with the man whose feelings about you define your entire self-concept.

One thing I learned through this one-on-one accountability was that I had to stop trying to outshine my man and start trying to create a dynamic in which we could both shine. In an unhealthy relationship, it seems that the one conflicts with the other. In a healthy relationship, the two build each other up without feeling that they're detracting from themselves as they do.

But often you need that truly honest female friend (sometimes brutally honest) to make sure you understand that. That's when you start to understand that your real place in the relationship is your Queenship!

Interestingly, while I had no idea that I belonged in a place like that, my gifts knew it completely. The things God put in me, the things designed to make me shine and grow and honor Him in my life, they knew exactly what I was supposed to be. That's why there was always so much internal conflict within my spirit. Because that knowledge was in there, and yet I failed to either recognize it or live with the expectation that it could ever be real.

But because I didn't recognize my gifts or the purpose for them, I wasn't finding my place and I wasn't flowing as God intended. Having gifts but leaving them untargeted and untapped is like receiving a mink coat – and wearing it around in the summer. Makes no sense, right? It's neither the time nor the right purpose. You might be walking around with your gift, but it's not prospering you or anyone else because you have no concept of what it's all about.

I think many of my failures in relationships with men were like that. I knew I had some gifts and that I could offer them to the men, but I didn't really understand what they were for. Because of that, I wasn't finding the spot in the relationship that would allow both of us to prosper. I didn't understand that serving each other shouldn't be a matter of intimidation, or two people playing politics with each other

— always trying to gain the upper hand.

A wise man once said, "Passion should never be mistaken for possession." Loving a man passionately, and having him love you just as passionately, does not mean he owns you. And a godly man wouldn't want to. He would want to flow *with* you. When a woman seeks to find herself and become the master of her own parade, some see that as arrogance. But it's not. Breaking out of that ritual cycle and understanding the royalty your gifts were intended to lead you to only make you a more powerful woman of God. They connect you to the identity He always intended for you.

A close female friend with whom I shared the crux of this chapter made an interesting comment: "There is a thin line between insanity and spiritual imagination."

The line is so thin because, in many ways, the two look alike. Without spiritual imagination, I can't envision myself as something greater than what I've been — because for that I need vision from God. But trusting God sometimes means stepping out and believing you can succeed in an area where you never have before. That might be interpreted as trying the same thing and expecting a different result. That's often what we call the definition of insanity. But spiritual insight tells you it's not a matter of your being doomed to failure. It's a matter of learning to do it God's way and trusting him.

My friend was right. There is a thin line between the two because you can convince yourself you've got spiritual insight when you're really just indulging your own delusions. Without staying close to God and being committed to studying the Scriptures, I don't know how a person could possibly tell the difference.

Once I understood I needed to stop sabotaging my womanhood, I needed God to reintroduce me to His plan for my life. I begin every day peeling the layers from my life that for years I allowed to become part of my journey — but that only led me farther from God. I enslaved myself by making approval from a man the most important thing in my life, and to my identity, instead of giving myself over only to God.

But there would be no more of that. I for once acknowledged that I am different, that I am beautiful, that I am smart and that I am special. I always had an understanding of these things, but I feared that if I really flowed in them, a man might not be comfortable flowing with me. He might feel less special than me, and making that man want me was always more important than flowing as God intended me to flow.

Fear is a crippling spirit that paralyzes one's ability to move forward. It led my life to fall apart, and when that happened I realized my roots were not deep enough, nor was my confidence strong enough. But I was full of contradictions. My perception of myself was both weak and tenacious, all at the same time. I was constantly fighting myself.

Finally, I was ready for that to be over – to conquer all this and become a conduit to change. I was ready to evolve, to understand and to pray to God. I hoped He would salvage my marriage, but if not, I prayed that He would at least salvage me.

The trustworthy female friend who can help you stay accountable on all this is not easy to find. You shouldn't trust that role to just anyone. But if you need that person in your life, then God knows you need her, and He will bring her to you. Take full advantage and be fully honest, lest you fall back into the traps that previously kept you from blossoming fully into the woman God always intended you to be.

Chapter Ten
On the Other Side of Ugly

"I can't promise you a perfect relationship, but what I can promise you is that as long as we're trying, I'm staying..." – Unknown Author

There may come a time when your relationship will experience a season of ugly!

I've long believed that someone should write a book to tell women what to do after the nest is empty, the disconnect is gone, and he is doing all the right stuff – yet you still feel empty from all the loads of life, and the responsibility of all the hats you're expected to wear. What happens when your well is dry at home, but the water you desire is in another vessel?

I touched this woman in the previous section called "The Cheating Woman." I have noticed that when you pass 40, your sex drive will get stronger. It appears that's when the lion comes out in us. There are all types of brand new emotions that breed. You want to be adventurous and you desire to be loved on another level.

This is the moment when you realize you are, or have been, deprived of something you have always desired. You've chosen to live in his normal, but quietly in your *abnormality*, you feel smothered by lust and desire and passion. I have recently had several conversations with women who are going through a "sneak moment" because the spontaneity in the marriage is depleted. Then doors open within yourself, and you start wondering how something new feels in your life.

In your husband's mind everything is copasetic, but we as women can go through ugly times in which we feel we are done with one and in with someone else. What happens when your vagina is dry for your spouse, but a running faucet with your maintenance man?

That is what we will call him. Cute, isn't it? He's "the maintenance man." He is a man that comes and makes some adjustments to your voids so you can function in some type of normal in your marriage. I have had so many women say that their cheating is a benefit for their spouses. They claim they are more loving, compassionate and lovable after they have been with their maintenance man.

Listen, sisters: we are evolving. Body and time are maturing you. Please do not allow time to mature your body, but leave your mind stuck in immaturities. Marriage is for grown people only. Children need to stay in the playground.

For me, the ugly season happened, and there were no rules to make it better for our relationship. I knew something was coming, but I never thought that ugly would come like this, and the bounce-back is hard. It's not easy to regain your footage in your marriage, and most importantly, in your own life.

I found myself feeling like I was bipolar, because one moment I wanted the good, bad and the ugly – and then in the next moment, I didn't. I was drained, my strength was gone. I tried, but I had to be honest about the fact that my energy was wasted. I still tried to hold on to possibilities, and my faith that God would turn my man's heart to maybe love me!

But I was afraid to believe that God could restore our relationship, because I wanted it to still be a testimony of reconciliation, so I could be what he needed and vice versa. The image of love with him was so numb in my soul that I wanted to go run and hide.

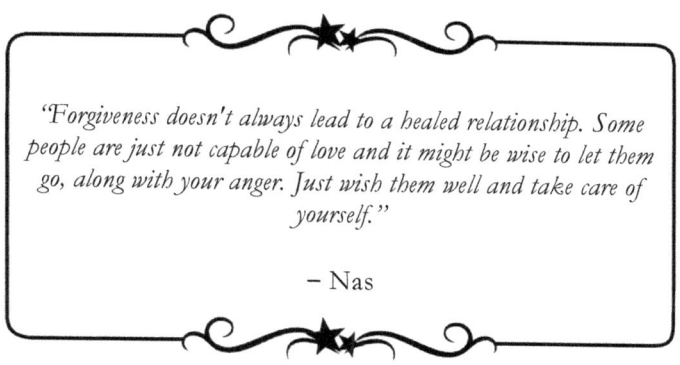

"Forgiveness doesn't always lead to a healed relationship. Some people are just not capable of love and it might be wise to let them go, along with your anger. Just wish them well and take care of yourself."

– Nas

But I was facing a fight. Did I really accept the ugly? How could this be? My love never stopped, but it shifted into a safe place. There are so many of us that are afraid of the ugly, but it is going to come and hopefully it will not take the form of adultery.

I wanted to move forward from the ugly and find counseling for us all. In the midst of all these imperfections, I still wanted to make love happen between us.

There are ways to get through the ugly, but it's easy to give yourself over to temptation. I found this out the hard way. In fact, I experienced both ends of it. Once I realized that my husband had cheated on me, it flared a lot of emotions.

For me, it brought back a dynamic of brokenness like never before. Trust went out the window, and for me it was a constant battle in the back of my mind. Did he ever really close the door? These were my questions in the midst of me trying to work it out:

1. Did he love her?
2. What did she provide that I did not?
3. How did he learn how to do something different sexually?
4. Are they still together or just taking a break?
5. And the list goes on and on...

If you suspect something, get your information first before you confront him. Never give them space to lie, and don't confront just with assumption! I had to protect myself, my children and my life. This ugly became uglier, and in the midst of all the passivity that he was giving to me, I had to swallow a reality pill: He wanted to be with the other woman. But I was so determined to keep my focus, no matter how hard it became, until I got that release in my soul to walk away.

I was always going to be a free-willed victim of this. I had to embrace that I deserve to be loved, and I could not wrap my mind around his statement to me: "She never meant anything."

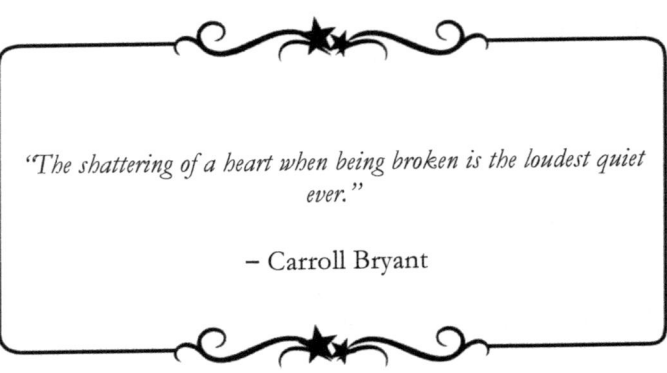

"The shattering of a heart when being broken is the loudest quiet ever."

– Carroll Bryant

I had to work out: Either we were going to be together

or this was over. If you made it and your marriage survived, thank you for continually showing that marriage can survive, and there are options on the other side of the ugly.

It takes two participants to regain the love, trust and true identity of your marriage. I learned that no one has the final say. Don't pray for a miracle in your marriage even as you expect grace to cover you in your affair. One of them has to go!

I had to survive this transition with or without him, and I believe that not only do we allow people to abuse us but we can abuse ourselves by choosing to stay in a relationship that tolerates and continuously brings our womanhood to complete devastation.

Love yourself more! If you are going to stay through the ugly, learn. If you leave because of the ugly, learn! Never waste an opportunity to know more about yourself. I often say that it's in the worst place of my life where I become the greatest.

Chapter Eleven

Sex on Another Level

We need to have a conversation about sex. And I'm not just talking about orgasms (although I *am* talking about that). I'm talking about sex on a whole other level, and about the trouble you are guaranteed to get into when you try to recreate that experience outside your marriage.

You may think you know your body pretty well, but I'm going to share some things that might enlighten you. And you might think you know your inner soul, but in my experience a lot of sisters don't understand the link between the two – and they certainly don't understand the problems they can inflict on their souls by making the wrong choices with their bodies.

So let me pose a question to you women who have cheated, and maybe are still cheating: How did you get so comfortable with what you're doing? And why do you find it shocking that you keep going back? That it feels like your lover's penis is a goody box, while your spouse has become predictable and boring?

You realize something, right? You gave your lover the

secret. You told him everything your husband isn't doing. And then you gave him the flirt you lost years ago with your husband. He allowed you to taste the desire you have longed for in your marriage, but that you were afraid to pursue with your husband because you didn't want to break his ego.

Nothing could devastate a man more than to find out he is not pleasing his wife sexually – that you're just going through the motions. It's never made sense to me that women can talk so openly with other women about their sexual desires, but they can't talk to their spouses about it. Maybe it's because it can be such a touchy subject. It could easily go like this:

"You know what I would really like? This . . ."

"Are you saying you're not happy with what we do now?"

"That's not what I'm saying."

"Well that's what it sounds like! What's wrong with what we do now?"

"Nothing, I would just like . . ."

"So you're unhappy that we haven't done that?"

You see what I mean, right? Maybe you've been there. Or maybe you haven't even tried to have this conversation because you thought it would go this way. So you complain to your sisters but you don't ever talk to your spouse about it. And eventually it becomes such a point of separation between you and him that the only way you think you can find satisfaction is with some other man.

Pretty soon, you're a beast with that other man, but you're Minnie Mouse with your spouse. You've got this unrevealed, untapped and unrequested passion that you're getting from someone other than your husband, and the truth is that you never even gave your husband the chance to give it to you.

If you told your husband how it really is, you would feel something about yourself. And you know what? You should let that happen. You should release yourself. Sex is a beautiful thing God made – and God set some definite parameters for how, and when, and under what circumstances, and with whom, it's to be enjoyed. When you enjoy it in this way, He will bless the experience in a wonderful way. When you start thinking you have to go outside God's parameters to get satisfaction, you're not just betraying your spouse. You're failing to trust God, because you don't believe He can make it awesome within your marriage.

I have talked to plenty of women who are happy in their marriages, but a certain turn in their lives they find themselves desiring more. Obviously this is not all married women, but we need to be honest about the fact that it does happen. Many women are very happy about the general strength of their families, but in the course of serving as the glue for the family, they lose themselves. Others lose their sense of need when they become empty-nesters. It's a difficult adjustment. Spouses don't always think or plan for what they'll do when the kids have left the house. They're just caught up in raising them. They don't even really get to know each other outside the duties of the house and the children.

When affairs occur after many years of marriage, it's often because couples failed to keep things fresh – emotionally, intimately, sexually – during the intensive years of raising children, tending to a house and so on.

There is also the heightened sex drive that hits many women when they get into their 40s. You can call it "Let Me See If I Still Have It Syndrome." But they want some fresh excitement, and one way to get it is to see if you can still interest men by flirting. It's no big deal, you tell yourself. You're just going to throw some bait out there and see if anyone nibbles. That's all you're going to do.

That's trouble! Once you've got a bite, are you sure you're going to be satisfied? Are you sure you don't want to take it to the next level? Flirt a little more? Touch a little? See how he responds to you? If you're bored with your routine of many decades, what can you do about that? Here's a man who is glad to give you attention. You can always go get some from him.

If you don't realize where this can lead, you're kidding yourself. That new, different, fresh experience you've been wanting sexually? Because of that heightened sex drive you're feeling? What could be fresher than a new man? What could be more exciting? And you can justify it, too, by telling yourself that your husband won't be receptive to your desires.

Of the women I've known who went in this direction, some don't even feel remorse. They say the sex was so mind-blowing that it just kept them going back. But I can tell you that women can't handle this on an emotional level. We're not wired like men. We get too involved on an emotional level. You're kidding yourself if you think you can have hot sex with your BOTS (boy on the side), then come home and sex your spouse — all the while seeing the images of Option B playing in your head.

That's not even real love! It's counterfeit love at best. It's straight-up lust at worst. The only thing that gives you hope of getting out of this mess is God's grace.

By the way, don't kid yourself into thinking sex is physical. Sex is mental. That man who's rocking your world right now is reading you mentally. He knows what you're not getting from your spouse, so it's very easy for him to send you home smiling.

Men are hunters, and a good hunter is both sneaky and observant. Men can give a woman a safe space, with all the spontaneity they want, and then sit back and observe her details. And because he understands those details, she will give him the world. This is why we need to be a little more honest than all those books and seminars that tell you to just cut off the affair, just like that. I'm not saying this isn't what you should do. Of course it is. But all that advice ignores the fact that it's extremely difficult to do it, and someone needs to show you how.

You've developed an appetite for your maintenance man, after all. You love the way he sexes you. The exotic challenge he presents to you is exciting. He kisses you like no one ever has. You're supposed to just drop everything and walk away from that? It's just that easy?

Of course it's not. The sex is so good because the emotion and the passion appeal to a neurotic place in you – something that either had never been opened before, or had not been tapped by your spouse in years. The woman who's been faking orgasms for years because her husband always ejaculates too quickly, and is now experiencing orgasmic sensations the likes of which she had only dreamed of before now . . . your advice to her is, hey, just cut it off?

"At some point after sex, we really need to determine whose fault this was."

– A popular e-card

The woman whose whole experience with her husband is that he goes in, gets what he's after and gets out – and she is now being caressed and held for the first time in an afterglow experience that's brand new? You're telling her to just walk away from that? Like it's that simple?

Yes, I know how wrong it is. But you're not even taking her challenge seriously if you're going to treat it like it's that easy. She's entered the Entanglement of Sexual Mind Control. What's that? That's a state in which she's become programmed to experience this level of release – the kind that only her maintenance man has ever been able to give her. She's having multiple orgasms with him, and every time it's over she starts thinking about when she's going to be able to come and experience it again.

Yes, I know this is artificial love. In fact, it's worse than that. It's a soul tie. It *feels* better than her husband because he seems so numb to what she needs, and the maintenance man seems so attuned to it. Now, even if you do go back to your husband, there's going to be pressure on him to perform like the maintenance man did. How's that going to work out?

There are all kinds of reasons it's difficult to walk away from the other man. But sisters, you have to understand: No matter how mind-blowing the sex may be, God is never going to honor it. Ever. The experience can only lead to one place, which is you lamenting everything and wondering how you got where you are.

And where you are is a red danger zone. If you can have sex with two men in one night – giving it to your husband just to appease him – then something internal in you is not clicking as it should. You need to seriously look at your commitment to your vows if you've gotten to this point. But I will tell you this: Don't walk away from your marriage over some turned-up, highly emotional sexual moment. It may be the best you've had in a long time, but is it worth your spirit, soul and body? Because that's what you've invested in your marriage all these years.

What you need to do is tell your husband what you're looking for. Over the years, anyone's body chemistry will change – and their needs will change with it. You need to first meet your own challenge and not be ashamed to address that. Then you need to adjust to the changes it brings on in you – and be honest with your husband about it.

Here's a real-life example. I know a woman who wanted her husband to start kissing her nipples. No big deal, you say? Sure, except for one thing: She'd told him 20 years ago that it turned her off when he did that, so he hadn't attempted it in all that time. Suddenly, with the kids grown and the house empty, she had realized it would promote a stronger orgasm and she wanted that.

Fortunately, in this case, her husband got past the initial confusion and was able to give her what she wanted. *And it was on.* She wasn't afraid to explore and address her own changes, and he wasn't afraid to make the adjustment.

I had the opportunity not long ago to meet a woman who showed women how to explore their bodies. I was a little taken aback by her method at first. She showed women how to do Kegel exercises, which involves the tightening of the vagina muscles.
Really?

But before long I decided to actually try it. These workouts are designed to give you a super-tight vagina, and you make it happen by squeezing your internal pelvic muscle mass. You can actually do it inconspicuously, so it doesn't matter where you are or in what circumstance. By the way, it's not true that too much sex gives you too loose a vagina. There are all kinds of other things that affect that, of which childbirth is only one. But yes, it's possible to tighten it again.

This is not to say that you should believe everything you hear people say about the female body. I have a very stupid friend, and I will spare him the humiliation of my telling you his name, but he claims he was told by a prostitute that what women need to do is take a both in hot water with a cup full of vinegar. Once I stopped laughing, I simply prayed that no woman was duped into trying such a humiliating thing.

Men have all kinds of misinformed ideas about women. I recently found an interesting post on dailydot.com, which really gets into things men think they know, and things women wish they knew. Here are the five items it shared:

1. Women can tell when men are doing something they saw in a porno. And guys, seriously, what works for the camera doesn't necessarily work for us.

2. Endurance is overrated. Yes, it's nice when it lasts longer than 60 seconds, but the vagina's ability to keep self-lubricating is not unlimited. Your accomplishments are very impressive but sometimes for us marathon sex is more of a duty than a joy.
3. We actually do know what will get us to orgasm. You might try asking, although the time to ask is probably not *during* sex.
4. "Getting there" can be more trouble than it's worth. Women like orgasms, but those who have trouble getting there don't necessarily want to endure a man's endless attempts to bring one forth. She might even be enjoying the sex regardless.
5. Our bodies are very sensitive when aroused, so be gentle. Or as one person put it, "That's a clitoris, not an elevator button."

The five points above don't necessarily apply to every woman, of course. But that's the point. All of our bodies are different, and they change all the time. If the sex in your marriage seems redundant to you, maybe it's because your husband doesn't know how you're changing. You need to tell him.

You don't want him sensing that he needs to come up with something different, and looking to pornography to get ideas. That's not real love. It's not even real sex! It's a perversion, and nothing he picks up from it is going to edify you. So tell him what you want. Even if it's a change from what you've said in the past, you can only help yourself and him by being open about it.

There are all kinds of things you can do to keep things exciting and satisfying. You can add a little music (and it doesn't have to be gospel music, sisters!), you can light some candles, you can try some romance oils . . . you will discover what works for you. Kiss him differently, and tell him to do the same to you. Try longer foreplay routines. Try wearing something sexy to get things started. Try role play. But remember, it all starts with mental intimacy. That comes before you two even touch each other. And that's why the sex you went for outside your marriage can never edify you like you hoped. It simply doesn't come with the life commitment that's been dedicated to love.

So if you're still wondering how you can handle breaking up with your maintenance man, let me leave you with this: What you think you could only get from him, you can and will get from God if you only give Him a chance. It's God who belongs at the center of your marriage, not this other man. What he did to your va-jay-jay can never measure up to how God wants to bless what you and your husband do to each other's hearts. And you realize: God is always watching you when you make love. If He can't honor what He's seeing, then you need to stop what you're doing.

Disconnect from that soul tie, no matter how hot and passionate it seems. Throwing away the marriage God wants to bless for something that's purely physical will always hurt you in the end. And if you don't believe me, here's 11 different translations of Hebrews 13:4 that prove it:

KJ21
Marriage is honorable in all, and the bed undefiled; but whoremongers and adulterers God will judge.

ASV
Let marriage be had in honor among all, and let the bed be undefiled: for fornicators and adulterers God will judge.

AMP
Marriage is to be held in honor among all [that is, regarded as something of great value], and the marriage bed undefiled [by immorality or by any sexual sin]; for God will judge the sexually immoral and adulterous.

AMPC
Let marriage be held in honor (esteemed worthy, precious, of great price,

and especially dear) in all things. And thus let the marriage bed be undefiled (kept undishonored); for God will judge and punish the unchaste [all guilty of sexual vice] and adulterous.

BRG
Marriage is honorable in all, and the bed undefiled: but whoremongers and adulterers God will judge.

CEB
Marriage must be honored in every respect, with no cheating on the relationship, because God will judge the sexually immoral person and the person who commits adultery.

CJB
Marriage is honorable in every respect; and, in particular, sex within marriage is pure. But God will indeed punish fornicators and adulterers.

CEV
Have respect for marriage. Always be faithful to your partner, because God will punish anyone who is immoral or unfaithful in marriage.

DARBY
[Let] marriage [be held] every way in honour, and the bed [be] undefiled; for fornicators and adulterers will God judge.

DLNT
Let marriage be honored by all, and the bed undefiled. For God will judge the sexually-immoral-ones and adulterers.

CHAPTER TWELVE

The Day I Decided to Die on the Inside

My Urge to Inflict Emotional Revenge

I tried to kill my husband. I almost succeeded. His blood was everywhere. It would have been nothing to finish him off. I wanted to;
but then I stopped; because the Lord had other plans for both of us.

Actually putting this incident in this book was not an easy decision, but if I'm serious about everything I've been trying to say from the first chapter to this last one, then you need to know about it. At some point, you might be in the same position I was. You might discover that a man, who had betrayed you, only to see you take him back, had gone ahead and betrayed you again.

You might be filled with rage to the point of wanting revenge. And you might find yourself wanting to disregard everything you know about how wrong it is to physically assault another person – because you're so filled with rage.

Stop. You owe it to yourself to think instead of messing up your life and everything you worked so hard to accomplish. There is so much more about you still worth living for. Preferably I chose me, I did. Listen to me, *Run*, get out of there before you do something that lands you in prison, where you will be no good to yourself or your children.

I used to have visions of what I would do if I ever caught my husband having an affair. They weren't pretty visions, but I had them. When I hear now about women who have been hurt so badly that they want to kill their husbands, I can no longer shake my head and act like it's unimaginable. When that pain circled to me, I felt like I was going to die.

I used to say that women who could last through infidelity were super amazing. Then the pump was on my foot. Now I know it has nothing to do with being amazing. It's simply love – the kind you maintain in sickness and in health, for better or for worse. Because you can't possibly be amazing enough to stand in the face of that much hurt. No one can.

After I first learned that my husband had been unfaithful, I hurt terribly, and yet parts of me still loved him. I thought that maybe, if we could work it out, we could become that one encouraging couple that provides such a great example for their friends and families – the one that had walked through the storm and conquered it.

But as I prayed, and cried, I still filed divorce papers. When they were served to him, he insisted he didn't want a divorce. He pleaded with me to try to reconcile.

I knew this would take hard work, emotional healing, restoration of trust, honesty and most of all counseling. But I was willing to give it a try. He moved back in with the family and the weird adjustment began. Whenever he touched me, I couldn't help but think about who else he'd been touching so recently.

But we had children, and I felt I should at least keep my heart open to the possibility. We started communicating again. We tried to get back in the groove. I tried to be intimate with him. But it wasn't working, and I knew it. My heart wasn't down with the idea of fully giving myself to him. One night when I was trying to make it work with him sexually, I had to just stop and tell him I couldn't.

He kept trying, though. He'd be home every night by 9 p.m. He even gave me the password for his phone so I could look and see what was on there. I started to let my guard down – to believe that maybe I needed to do more to make this work.

I was trying hard to buy into that the night he came home with a scent on him – and I knew instantly that I'd been had. I felt nauseous. He smelled like sweat and sex. I wrestled with myself over the question of whether I should say something. At first, I didn't. But that night, when he touched me – when I was as close to him as I could possibly get – I unmistakably smelled *her*.

My rage was growing. I pretended to fall asleep at the same time he did, but as soon as I was sure he was sleeping I went over and got his phone. Remember, he had given me the password. Maybe he thought the mere act of giving me the password would breed so much trust that I would never actually use it. And maybe that would have been true, until I smelled the smell on him. I prayed that what I suspected was there would not, in fact, be there.

But it was. Everything. The pictures. The instant messages. The texts. None of it had stopped. I'd been played.

I looked over at him, my anger burning. That was it. I woke him up. He was stunned and delirious as I told him I had seen *everything* on his phone. And I went off.

First I grabbed a vase and hit him with it over and over. As glass shattered, his blood gushed. I didn't care. I had let this man back into my life and into my home – and my children's home – after he had been unfaithful. And this was what he did? As he lay there helpless, with no idea what was going to happen next, I made it clear that the beating had just begun. I would bash him with the now-shattered glass vase over and over again. I would have no mercy.

But then I stopped. As he waited to see what I was going to do next, I simply told him to leave. Needless to say, he did so quickly.

Only God could have stopped me from killing him that night, because I can tell you for real that I wanted to. And I was prepared to. But the Holy Spirit convicts us, and that night He convicted me. By the time he'd been gone about two hours, I just broke down and cried. I felt so stupid and hurt.

Oh, and I talked to the other woman! You might wonder why I would do that, but I had some specific questions I wanted answered. And I got my answers. It turns out I'd been presented as an insecure, older, deranged woman. This was who she thought I was, and I guess that's part of what she used to justify her involvement with him.

Even as I talked to her, there was still a part of me that wanted them both dead. But the Ane who listens to God knew better. After all, I'd been in her position, and I knew what that scrutiny felt like. No. I really did not want to subject her to it.

Also, I realized that I was dealing with a sickness, insecurity, a life of deception that really wasn't even about me. I prayed that God would touch his heart. I decided to love him, but I had to categorize that love in a different way. I had to recognize the signs of abuse and understand that I could only be sure of change in one person – and that was me.

I'm sure that some of you are horrified to read what I've told you in this chapter, and to realize that it was actually a Christian person doing these things. Guilty. Hurt does not go any easier on us because of our faith. Rage is a betrayed person's friend, and revenge is what we often use to warn the betrayer: You might not make it out of this fight alive.

I would love to tell you a story about how, because I'm a Christian, I made no mistakes and crossed no lines and committed no sin – regardless of the things that were happening in my life. But I have yet to meet the Christian who can honestly tell that story, and it certainly isn't me.

I still love God. I'm still saved by the grace of Jesus, and this book is the story of why I need that grace. Still, if you don't think I am, *pray for me*. I appreciate it.

Had I not loved God, it wouldn't have mattered to me that He made it clear that it was *not* His will for me to do what I wanted to do. What's more, He showed me that this was not His will for me in terms of finding love in my life. He taught me not to judge all men by the failure of one.

I remember standing in my closet and asking God what had happened. Deep in my heart I heard His answer: "His pain wouldn't let Me heal him."

With that, I believed the best choice I could make was to leave him. I felt like this quote:

"It's almost like you had it planned, it's like you smiled and shook my hand and said, 'Hey, I'm about to screw you over, big time.'"

— MoZella

Had I listened to myself, I'd be in prison right now. Someone else would be raising my three children. That would have been a terrible tragedy. By releasing him, I gained myself back. I felt a lot of fear and pain over the prospect of once again becoming a single mother. Of feeling lonely. Of the shame associated with divorce. If this would be my new normal, it sounded awfully old – and not good.

I had agreed to the judge's request that we attempt a 60-day reconciliation period, but obviously we didn't make it. I felt like a failure. But I had to acknowledge that my path was not the same as my friends' paths, and I also had to trust that God could restore anything.

He could have restored this marriage if both of us had been in agreement to commit ourselves to it, but that was not the case. His heart was no longer with me, and that hurt, but I wasn't doing myself any good pretending it wasn't true. I knew it was.

I should have recognized the signs right away. They were there. I never really knew this man I had married. I didn't react to the warning signs, and I didn't deal well with reality. Dr. Laura often says, "When someone shows you who they are, work with that – not your hopes or fantasies."

Ultimately, I had to deal with who he really was – not who I wished he would become. I filed the divorce papers four days later. I took a deep breath and said; OK, now I would have to trust God with this path – this journey to healing. I can't help that he does not want me. I can't honestly tell you my love for him completely ended – but with his frailties I could not be responsible for his refusal to let God heal him.

Now, as I embark on my journey back to me, I understand that I cannot afford to attract this kind of man again. That means I have to *heal me*. It starts with forgiving him, because I can't heal if I hate. That's the fastest way to die emotionally, spiritually and physically. I want to heal, and I thank God that I am willing to walk this journey of healing and rediscovery. I died internally that night; I had to, so that I could find myself again.

My plight may not be yours. I hope it's not. But I want you to know there is life after divorce. I also want you to know that, if you decide not to walk away, you will need to control your anger. Otherwise you can look forward to prison ministry, and believe me, it's not worth it.

So before you snap or go off, stop. Listen to God. You have too much to lose, and it's all more valuable than you can possibly imagine. So take your life back and live.

I did.

> Breakups hurt, but losing someone who doesn't respect and appreciate you is actually a gain, not a loss.

"If You Can Hang in There, Your Marriage is Worth Fighting for."

The End

www.ingramcontent.com/pod-product-compliance
Lightning Source LLC
Chambersburg PA
CBHW050111170426
43198CB00014B/2534